ARCHITECTURAL DESIGN

EDITORIAL OFFICES:
42 LEINSTER GARDENS, LONDON W2 3AN
TEL: 0171-402 2141 FAX: 0171-723 9540

EDITOR: Maggie Toy
EDITORIAL TEAM: Iona Spens (Senior Editor), Stephen Watt
ART EDITOR: Andrea Bettella
CHIEF DESIGNER: Mario Bettella
DESIGN: Phil Kirwin

CONSULTANTS: Catherine Cooke, Terry Farrell, Kenneth Frampton, Charles Jencks, Heinrich Klotz, Leon Krier, Robert Maxwell, Demetri Porphyrios, Kenneth Powell, Colin Rowe, Derek Walker

SUBSCRIPTION OFFICES:
UK: VCH PUBLISHERS (UK) LTD
8 WELLINGTON COURT, WELLINGTON STREET
CAMBRIDGE CB1 1HZ
TEL: (0,223) 321111 FAX: (01223)

USA AND CANADA: VCH PUBLISHERS INC
303 NW 12TH AVENUE DEERFIELD BEACH,
FLORIDA 33442-1788 USA
TEL: (305) 428-5566 / (800) 367-8249
FAX: (305) 428-8201

ALL OTHER COUNTRIES:
VCH VERLAGSGESELLSCHAFT MBH
BOSCHSTRASSE 12, POSTFACH 101161
69451 WEINHEIM
FEDERAL REPUBLIC OF GERMANY
TEL: 06201 606 148 FAX: 06201 606 184

CONTENTS

Ushida Findlay, Soft and
Hairy House, Tokyo

GUY BATTLE AND CHRISTOPHER McCARTHY
MULTI-SOURCE SYNTHESIS
Sculpting with Energy

The engineer's brief is to maximise the use of energy, materials and skill for the benefit of all. And yet most of the engineering that goes into the creation of our built environment is carried out too late. It is the strategic decisions, made early in the design process, that have the greatest influence on the environmental efficiency and success of urban proposals. Precise and cogent engineering analysis of a full range of strategic options is essential for use by everyone who is instrumental in shaping the built environment.

Rapid and simple analysis tools are needed to assess the implications of proposals at an early stage; and they need to be fast enough to allow multiple iteration, allowing a large number of options to be considered. In the early stages of designing a building, decisions on massing and orientation can have considerable influence on the eventual energy consumption of the building. Although later design decisions will also have an effect, it is important for the architect and client to be able to consider this aspect right at the start of the design process. Here we present the initial analysis that we have carried out on two projects, one in London and one in Hong Kong, which in their very different qualities reflect the differences of climate and urban density in the two cities.

Responsive Energy Modelling in London
This project, with Terry Farrell and Company, demonstrates the use of an amended version of the Lighting and Thermal Method, first developed by Cambridge Architectural Research, for energy massing analysis. When linked to a spreadsheet, used with a desk top computer modelling program, the method provides a rapid comparative assessment of a range of proposals.

The Method works by calculating energy consumption figures for different zones of a building, based upon the following factors:
- Local climatic conditions
- Orientation of facades
- Area and type of glazing
- Overshadowing from adjacent buildings
- The inclusion of atria
- Occupancy and vacation patterns
- Lighting levels

The energy consumption and carbon dioxide emissions figures produced represent good practice, though they are not absolute, for it is impossible to predict actual occupancy patterns. Their primary value is to provide a comparison between different building options.

The objective of the computer energy modelling was not to lead the masterplan but gauge the potential energy consumption of each massing option. The first option filled the whole site with building form. As would be expected, this generated the highest energy demand as it requires artificial lighting, mechanical ventilation and cooling in all areas for most of the year. Fragmenting the building to 40 x 40 metre blocks did not reduce the energy demands by a significant amount as they were too deep to naturally ventilate and had poor daylight penetration. Thinner 12 to 15 metre wide buildings with the main facades on a south-north orientation, with atria and pre-heat to ventilation, generated the lowest energy demands due to increased daylight potential and the ability to use mixed-mode systems with natural ventilation in the mid-season condition.

Energy and the Community in Hong Kong
Frei Otto and Buckminster Fuller both speculated about cities in bubbles, as seen in their proposals for Arctic City and for Manhattan. While the concept of entire cities in artificial environments is likely to be undesirable, the principle has yet to be applied fully to buildings. In Hong Kong – due to the massive expansion of retail service requirements – podium levels are rising every year, to the point where they may eventually submerge the existing skyscrapers. In response to this condition, we have developed an advanced eco-tower proposal for the Hong Kong community with Terry Farrell and Company. The proposal consists of a single one-kilometre tower generated from a radial arrangement of buildings. The axial and stability loads are carried by the peripheral service cores, which also act as collectors for solar power. Between the cores an active facade system controls the quantity of light and heat energy allowed into the development, creating a controlled environ-

The scale of the proposal enables the tower to create an acceptable artificial 'external' environment using ambient energy sources such as wind, solar radiation, and pressure and temperature differences with height. The radial arrangement of the blocks creates an artificial enclosure with a maximum number of building facades shaded from direct sun at any time; the height of the building enables it to take advantage of the dramatic variations in climatic conditions over its height – including a six degree temperature variation – to drive a high-pressure stack providing ventilation. The surface of the cores and active facade are able to absorb a maximum amount of solar energy via photovoltaics. Thus the desired artificial climate is generated within which the offices operate, and they may be naturally ventilated throughout the year.

Further analysis will involve looking at the building layout to optimise solar shading and daylight penetration, and analysing the shape of the entire envelope; while a cylinder creates maximum volume with minimum surface area, a particular orientation of ellipse may provide a better response to the sun path.

Futures

With the new release of SimTower, the follow-up to SimCity by Maxis, we are provided with a basic tool to commence a conversation with the Hong Kong community about towers of this nature, providing an understanding of the driving forces behind such a proposal, and what the tower might be like to live and work in. The tower design will thus become an example of the use of the full range of new engineering design tools.

The authors would like to thank Robert Webb for his assistance in the preparation of this article. The discussion of tower design is continued in the next issue of Architectural Design, *which focuses on the skyscraper.*

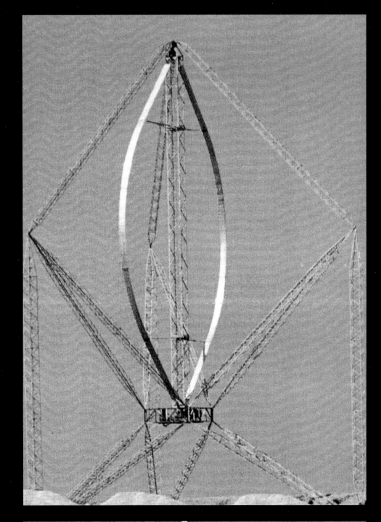

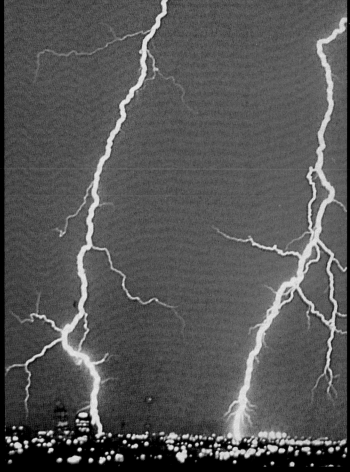

FROM ABOVE: Vertical-axis wind turbine; lightning strikes above the city

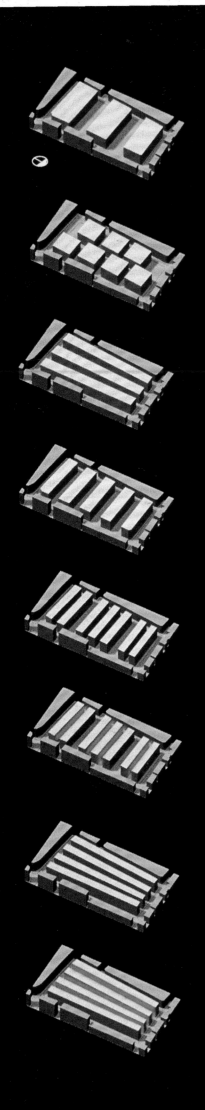

Energy Use 642 kWh/m^2

| Lighting | Heating | Ventilation and Cooling |

Carbon Dioxide Emissions 411 kg/m^{2}yr

Energy Use 634 kWh/m^2

Carbon Dioxide Emissions 393 kg/m^{2}yr

Energy Use 607 kWh/m^2

Carbon Dioxide Emissions 312 kg/m^{2}yr

Energy Use 650 kWh/m^2

Carbon Dioxide Emissions 327 kg/m^{2}yr

Energy Use 220 kWh/m^2

Carbon Dioxide Emissions 89 kg/m^{2}yr

Energy Use 112 kWh/m^2

Carbon Dioxide Emissions 65 kg/m^{2}yr

Energy Use 245 kWh/m^2

Carbon Dioxide Emissions 99 kg/m^{2}yr

Energy Use 124 kWh/m^2

Carbon Dioxide Emissions 88 kg/m^{2}yr

Energy massing studies for a central London site, showing option tested and resulting energy and carbon dioxide emissions. The sixth and the eighth options have atria used as ventilation pre-heat; OPPOSITE, FROM ABOVE: Visualisation of daylight penetration and mid-season ventilation in the resulting scheme: Atria act to bring daylight into the building and, utilising a wind-driven stack effect, draw warm exhaust air out of the building

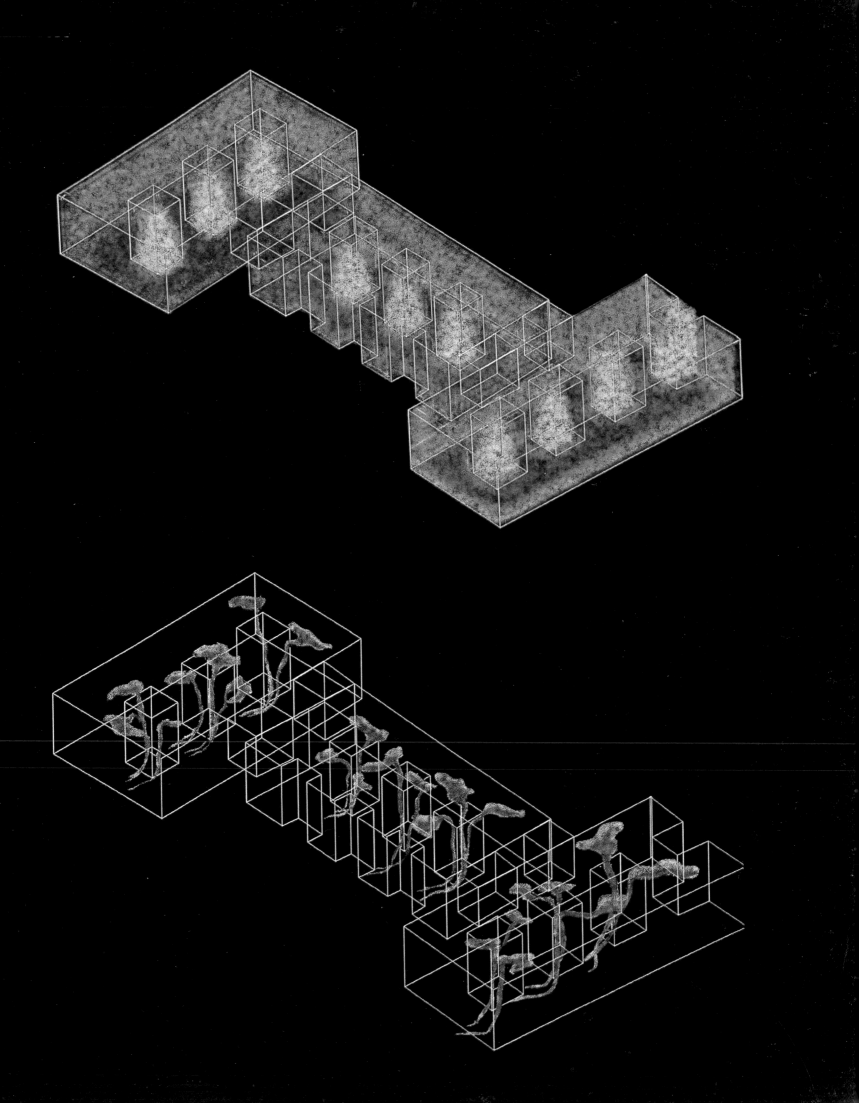

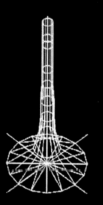
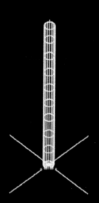

Summer Day
Average Temperature (°C)

Summer Day
Humidity (RH%)

Summer Day
Wind speed (sheltered direction)

Summer Day
Wind speed (various directions)

Summer Day
Noise (dB)

Summer Day
Pollution

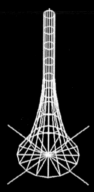
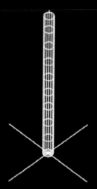

Summer Night
Average Temperature (°C)

Summer Night
Humidity (RH%)

Summer Night
Wind speed (sheltered direction)

Summer Night
Wind speed (various directions)

Summer Night
Noise (dB)

Summer Night
Pollution

June 210900

June 211200

June 211500

June 21 1800

September 21 0900

September 21 1200

September 21 1500

September 21 1800

December 21 0900

December 21 1200

December 21 1500

December 21 1800

The Hong Kong Tower: three-dimensional plots of environmental conditions over the 1,000m height of the

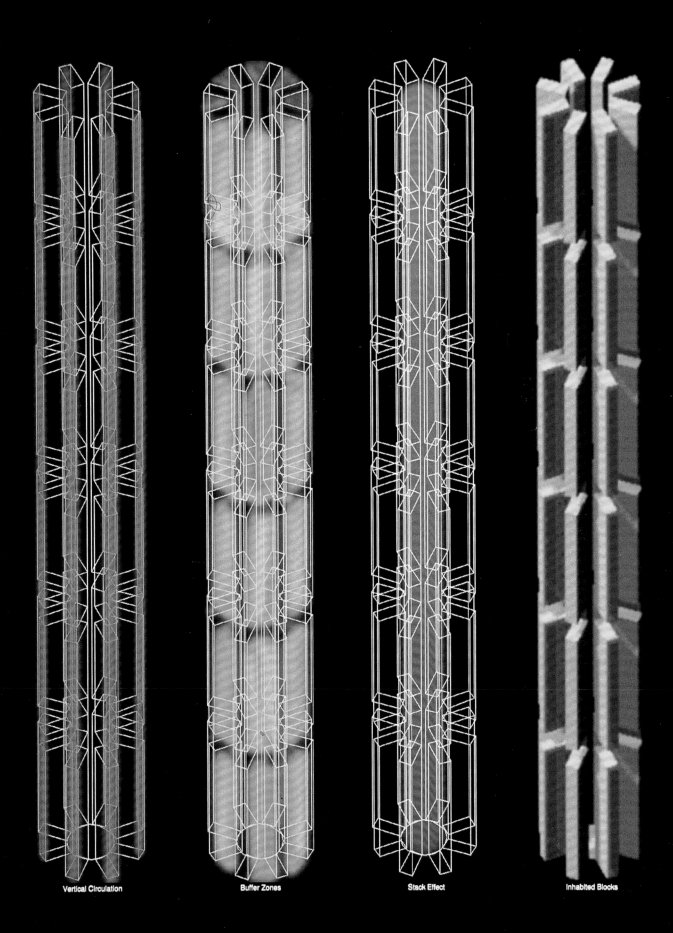

Vertical Circulation Buffer Zones Stack Effect Inhabited Blocks

Vertical circulation; buffer zones; stack effect; inhabited blocks

ABOVE: Nambikkai Foundation
for the Deaf, Tamil Nadu, main
building with bottle jali; BELOW:
Centre for Development Studies,
Trivandrum, Kerala: internal view
of secondary stair, lit by jali;
exterior looking towards the
decahedron library

LAURIE BAKER IN INDIA

FRED CAMPBELL

The belief that we all have individual gifts that are given for the benefit of all is enlarged upon in Francis Dewar's book *Live for a change*. Laurie Baker is an example of this. He is unusual: an Englishman among Indians; an architect among builders, doctors, academics and civil servants. Baker, now seventy-eight, was born in England in 1917. He studied at the Birmingham School of Architecture and became an associate of the Royal Institute of British Architects. With the outbreak of war his pens were put away, and being of a Quaker background he joined a mobile surgical team as an anaesthetist. Some time later, he found himself in Western China helping in the treatment and control of leprosy.

In 1944, en route back to Britain, he was detained three months in Bombay, awaiting a boat home, where he met Ghandi. After only a brief spell back in England, he returned to India and was married in 1948 to Elizabeth Jacob, a doctor from Kerala in the south. They went to live in a remote area of the Himalayas where they built a home, a hospital, and some schools. They stayed until development crept up on them and then upped sticks and settled in an upland area of Kerala, again building a home and a hospital. Come 1970, the Bakers had moved one last time to Trivandrum, the capital of Kerala, a city spread out on ridges of palm groves.

It was here that we met in 1991, having heard of him at the office where I was working in Madras. Told that he was unwell, I went to meet his son, whereupon Baker himself appeared. Four years on, I recall his affability. He said that he only drew what was necessary, for planning, and thereafter worked daily on site and made adjustments as the building went up; for example, making a window opening where there was a good view. One of his design handbooks points out that plans need not always be square or rectangular.[1] Taking into consideration trees on the site, a well, sloping ground, an outcrop of rocks, a beautiful distant view, the direction of the wind and rain, a plan that responds to such aspects is unlikely to fit into a square: 'What is so sacred about a square anyway?' he asks.

A major concern involves making the building as cost effective as he can conceive, and this has resulted in some ingenious methods of construction and detailing. Rudimentary insights involve the benefits of the 'filler slab', for example, based upon engineering principles remembered from the Birmingham School. The filler slab reduces the volume of concrete required with the addition of a sandwich of roof tiles, making a lighter cheaper slab, with better insulation. For brick walls, the 'rat trap' bond is apparently 25 per cent cheaper than other bonds like English and Flemish. Heavy and costly lintels are avoided with brick arches, corbelled brickwork, or concrete lintels linked with bricks. Doors and windows can be frameless and furniture built in. Well finished brickwork removes the necessity of a plaster finish, cutting 10 per cent from the total cost. Wastage is kept to a minimum, using broken bricks as bats in walls and floors. The use of brick 'jali' allows air to ventilate and cool interiors, an adaptation of an historical element. His approach is hugely practical, and lyrical too, in a light way. Was it not Louis Kahn who wrote that a brick wants to be an arch?

Another handbook written by Baker on the use of mud reveals his heartfelt attitude: '. . . it is a fact that something between twenty and thirty million families in our country do not have anything that can even remotely be called a home or a house or even a hut. So I wish that we had a collective national conscience about this and seriously, all of us, not just "the Government" should set about doing something about it so that this disgrace is removed.'[2]

Here is a man who has helped to build many hundreds of houses and influenced thousands more, plus some hospitals, schools, and institutions; an architect who has advised the Indian government on housing and extended his discipline into the medical and social spheres. Driven with a sense of purpose, Baker grasped his talents and put them to work. He has been met with fulfilment: 'Over a period of fifty years, and more, I have had a lot of enjoyment with bricks . . . Like most good things in life you have to get down to it and do it yourself to get real enjoyment and satisfaction.'[3]

He is an architect in the old fashioned way that in this country is hardly seen in the days of narrow career definitions. To be in exile has for Laurie Baker been an opportunity. For India, it has been a boon.

FROM ABOVE: Illustration by Baker of the manufacture of pressed earth blocks; Trivandrum Bus Station Information Centre before completion; Baker in 1991

1 *The Next Step Towards Getting a Laurie Baker Home*, HUDCO, Madras, India, 1989.
2 *Laurie Baker's Mud*, COSTFORD, Valapad, India, 1988.
3 *Laurie Baker's Brickwork*, ibid.

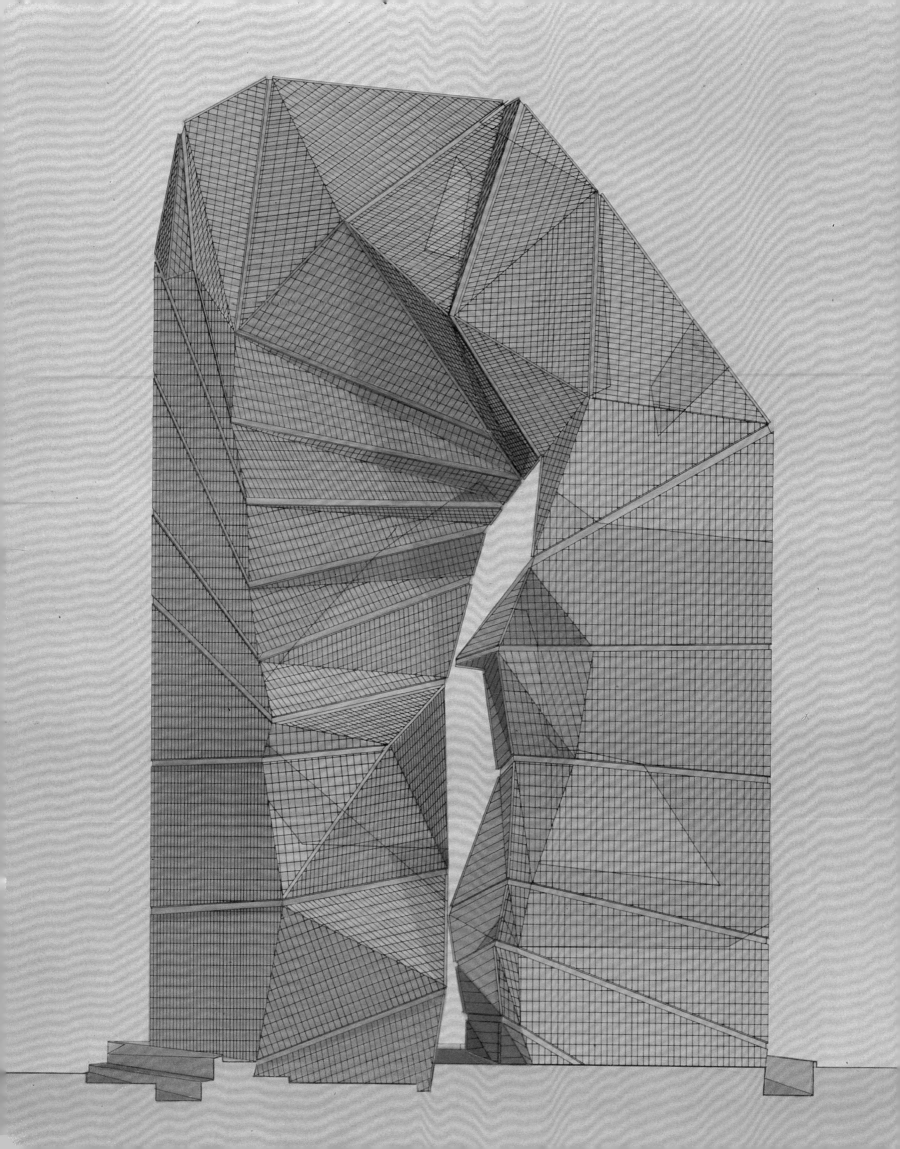

CHARLES JENCKS
AN ARCHITECTURE OF WAVES AND TWISTS

*Charles Jencks' recently published 'The Archi-
tecture of the Jumping Universe' (Academy
Editions, 1995) is a polemic in the tradition of
partisan manifestos which argues that the new
sciences of complexity and cosmology have
overturned the old Newtonian world view and
are ushering in a New World view based on
sudden emergence, self-organising systems
and 'jumps'. In this extract he explains one of
the nine basic aspects of the shift this is
causing in design – towards an architecture of
waves and twists.*

Why give so much emphasis to an
architecture of undulating forms? The
partial answer is that wave motion,
like nonlinearity, is so crucial and omnipresent
in nature. At a basic level, in the microworld of
quantum physics, the wave function of the atom
is as fundamental as the particulate aspect.
Every subatomic particle is both wave and
particle. Every object and human being is
composed of this bipolar unity, this double
entity. The wave aspect is masked to us,
however, because it is unobservable compared
to our relatively huge size.

Some physicists believe, moreover, that
thought is basically a wave phenomenon. This
is intuitively obvious; after all, an idea weighs
nothing, is contained all over the brain, is
stretched out like a wave, can travel near the
speed of light, and is changeable like an ocean
wave. Quantum waves also have, like thoughts,
paradoxical properties: unlike particles and
objects, they can tunnel through walls – a
miracle that happens in every television set.
A wave form is also the superposition of many
small waves and thus, like a thought, can
contain many contradictory states within itself
without collapsing. It is a truism of psychology
today to say that the self is constructed of
many contradictory parts (child self, parent
self, worker self, leisure self, and so on) just as
it is a truism to say we often have many contradictory thoughts struggling in our mind at once
– voices superimposed on each other and held
in suspension, just as a quantum wave is the
superposition of many smaller waves.

Quantum waves can add up, cancel, go
through each other, and be in several places at

once. In short, the wave form contains the
properties well known as 'quantum weirdness',
the paradoxical and essential mind-quality of
the universe. This is not the place to discuss
the extraordinary aspects of quantum mechan-
ics, but the wave form and function are so
basic and important in the universe that it is the
place to emphasize the fundamental place they
should have in architecture.

I have been particularly drawn to representing the strange phenomenon of the soliton
wave, because it shows the coherence of a
nonlinear feedback system, and something
approaching 'memory'. The Red Spot of Jupiter
is a soliton, as are the tidal bores that can
reach twenty-five feet in height and travel at a
constant speed for five hundred miles. Solitons
were first theorized by the Scottish engineer
John Scott Russell in 1834, after he had an
unusual experience while riding his horse along
the Union Canal near Edinburgh:

I was observing the motion of a boat which
was rapidly drawn along a narrow channel by a
pair of horses when the boat suddenly stopped
– not so the mass of water in the channel which
it had put in motion; it accumulated round the
prow of the vessel in a state of violent agitation,
then suddenly leaving it behind, rolled forward
with great velocity, assuming the form of a
large solitary elevation, a rounded, smooth and
well defined heap of water, which continued its
course along the channel apparently without
change of form or diminution of speed. I
followed it on horseback, and overtook it still
rolling on at a rate of some eight or nine miles
an hour, preserving its original figure some
thirty feet long and a foot to a foot-and-a-half in
height. Its height gradually diminished, and
after a chase of one or two miles I lost it in the
windings of the channel.

Russell's solitary wave, or soliton, keeps its
identity instead of dissipating, as do normal
waves because the smaller waves that consti-
tute it bounce back and reinforce the overall
shape and frequency. This feedback is the
reverse of turbulence. It is obviously balanced
on the delicate edge between order and chaos:
if the width or depth of the canal is varied
greatly, the resonance will not occur. Given the
coherence of such waves, they can do unusual

*OPPOSITE: Peter Eisenman, Max
Reinhardt Haus, project for Berlin,
1993. A prismatic architecture that
folds itself into a heterogeneous
landscape. Partly based on a
method of folding and various
sciences of complexity, this multi-
use building combines the
skyscraper, omni-center, triumphal
arch and Mobius strip into an
enigmatic mixture. The architect
states that he wishes to provide a
kaleidoscopic building that enfolds
difference into itself, symbolising
Germany and the future. He has
also spoken of it, in jest, as the
first non-phallic monument which
invaginates two phallic symbols
into each other. By breaking the
frame of the triumphal arch, and
box, the building does combine
inside and outside as intriguingly
as its combination of functions. But
as a paradoxical Mobius strip –
that is, a two-dimensional surface
with only one side – it symbolises
both the paradoxes of infinity and
contemporary cosmology. In a
Super-string universe the ultimate
model may be a Kline bottle
(three-dimensional version of a
Mobius strip). Thus a fresh image,
appropriate to its symbolic role,
and based on leading science: a
cosmogenic architecture.*

things, such as pass intact through each other. Or a high, thin, humpbacked soliton can overtake a short, fat one, combine for a while as a single wave, and then re-emerge, as if the two remembered their separate identities. Solitons have been found in such diverse systems as planetary atmospheres, crystals, plasmas, and nerve fibres, and have been created for such systems as superconductors and optical fibres.

In general they can be considered as focused energy waves, or coherent patterns. They can be represented in two basic ways: either as the travelling hump in a whiplash or as the twist in a flat strip, such as a leather belt. The second is 'topologically trapped' and can be eliminated only by an anti-twist. 'Humps' and 'twists' are two signs I have used, especially in a series of metal gates to represent the travelling of focused energy through the universe.

These show waves of energy moving from the points of focus, or structure – here the latch or hinges. They travel across the gate diagonally, giving a kind of visual energy that is accentuated by the alternation of solid and void, black and white, foreground and background. The twists appear almost absent, so the represented soliton seems to pass through the gate to the points that hold it, and where it opens. The latch is further focused by a twisted Mobius Strip, itself an endless form, and a spiral fossil, which also takes up the curvilinear geometry. Sometimes the soliton even travels, at least visually, into the stone wall. Thus natural and designed wave forms are merged.

I find depicting solitons compelling, not only because of their aesthetic energy but also because of their inspiration in a new science. They represent deeper aspects of the natural world that are just being discovered, and I believe architecture should always engage with such investigation. Even if it should not situate itself exclusively at the edge of knowledge, architecture needs always to be pushing the frontiers – not just of technology and materials, but of science and our understanding of ourselves. I believe we are most fascinated by this art when it is conveying something in a beautiful language that we did not know before. Perhaps this is because, of all definitions applied to us, we are 'the learning animal'. Our aesthetic enjoyment and pleasure in life are deeply tied to curiosity, adaptation, the will to discover new truths; and this drive has to be put at the center of a new philosophy.

Plato, Nietzsche and Freud were wrong – it is not immortality, power and sex which drives us (important as they may be) – but learning. The whole universe is trying to discover its own being, and we are at the forefront of this cosmic lust for knowledge.

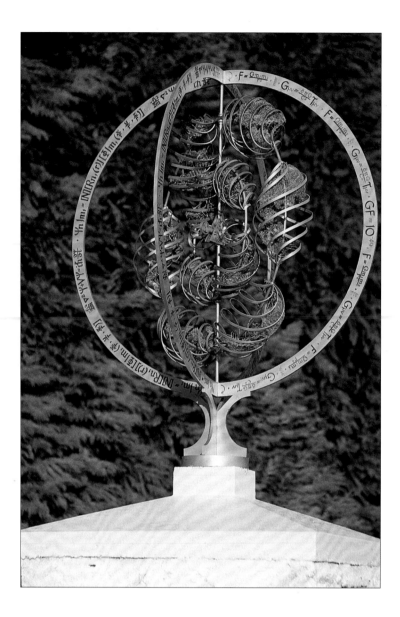

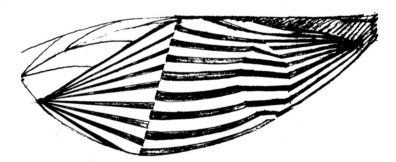

FROM ABOVE: Charles Jencks, Atom, showing first two coils of the wave and particulate aspect of the electron orbit. The basic organisational aspects – from trapped jumps to the mathematical unfolding of the wave – are represented in this atom turned in the wind; Garden Terrace. Four symmetry breaks represented: convergent lines, implied figures, positive/ negative reversals and visual ambiguity. Visual vibrations are akin to energy waves and interference patterns caused by waves

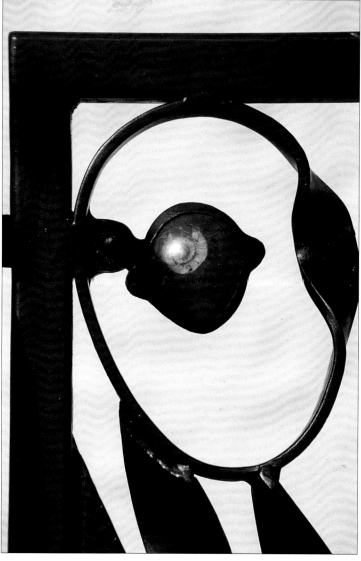

ABOVE: Wave Gate 2 and detail. Three pulses of energy, represented by twists, run through the metal towards the latch (fossil) and its spiral held inside a Mobius strip; BELOW: Wave Gates 4 and 5. Soliton waves represented travelling towards center latch and edge hinges punctuated by spiral fossils

FUTURE SYSTEMS
GALLERY FOR THE 21ST CENTURY

The international competition for a new Tate gallery of modern art at Bankside in London, won earlier this year by Swiss architects Herzog & de Meuron, gave rise to an imaginative range of designs seeking to animate the 8.5-acre site on the south bank of the Thames, opposite St Paul's and the City. The exterior of the disused power station by Giles Gilbert Scott (designer of the red telephone kiosk) will barely be altered by the winning scheme which retains as much as possible the internal spaces of the vast interior. This scheme by Future Systems in collaboration with Ove Arup & Partners is designed for the Bankside location though is not their entry for the competition. It sets out to conceptualise in built form the idea of a gallery for the twenty-first century. The description is followed by an environmental exhibition scheme for former East Germany.

The research element of the project is universal; the roof for example can be adapted for buildings with different geometries. The building is approached from the north via a footbridge, or from the river front, connecting to Southwark with a series of paths in parkland to the south. Three levels provide exhibition space, linked by ramps ensuring visible orientation within the galleries. Free-form floors aim to create a flexible layout for artworks beneath a great suspended roof which exploits natural daylight as the major source of illumination for exhibits. This avoids the reflected glare problems that occur with light from side windows and allows curators to arrange display spaces with more autonomy. The main exhibition walls are conceived as a natural extension of the floors, growing organically from them. Intermediate partitions can be placed at random.

Direct sun is excluded from gallery spaces by a passive system of light control: light enters from the northern parts of the sky through the orientation of a modular system of external shells whose outer, south-facing surfaces support photovoltaic panels to provide a free energy source. The glazing in each shell incorporates a colourless ultraviolet filter, absorbing light's most damaging wavelengths. Suspended fabric scales provide a second layer of light control: beneath each roof a white fabric scale shell diffuses incoming skylight for even illumination. These are replaced with more dense fabric for light sensitive works. For more directional light, diffusing scales can be

omitted completely. Supplementary electric lighting may be provided by linear fluorescent uplights which wash the white underside of the roof shells. Track-mounted tungsten halogen spotlights facilitate direct highlighting for specific works on display.

The roof is designed to maximise daylight but not to detract from the artworks. A lattice of steel cables, which act in tension, prevent the structure from buckling. The saddle form derived from a computer program imitating the behaviour of a soap bubble stretched between its curves. A floor supply air-conditioning system extracts air adjacent to the external surface and removes heat gain from the sun. Heat is then available in the central plant during sunny, cool periods and the roof construction acts as a buffer zone. Downdraught in the winter is combated by high levels of insulation in the shells and by giving profile to the underside of the roof with the fabric scales. Clear polycarbonate used for the extract ducts at roof level reduces the visual impact of the ductwork and visually separates it from the structure.

Harnessing energy and communicating environmentally friendly construction techniques to East European builders and the public was the driving force behind a complex designed by the Stuttgart based practice Unit A. This aims to conserve energy, promote the rational use of alternative energy sources and reduce emissions of methane and dioxides. It is planned for Zittau, an area known for brown coal mining and its ecological damage. Here, the form is determined by the hilly landscape of the site and oriented with maximum southern exposure to provide the most efficient use of solar energy. The interior structure is composed of four levels of concrete slab and column construction for flexible use. Running services are generated by solar energy and light is filtered through the membrane roof material aided by solar reflectors. Air circulation occurs through natural thermal ventilation. A motorised power station using plant oil provides less polluted energy. All the different energy systems control energy data used throughout the building. In response to increasing use of information technology in exhibition centres, these are visible on computer monitors found on a 'Teaching Path' walkway through green areas connecting the various levels.

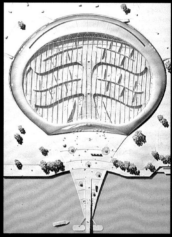

OPPOSITE: *Future Systems, Gallery for the 21st Century, montage and isometric; FROM ABOVE: Gallery model; Unit A, Centre for Environmentally Friendly Construction, model*

CARDIFF BAY OPERA HOUSE
ZAHA HADID

Changes follow the confirmation of Zaha Hadid's £47 million project as the winning design of the Cardiff Bay Opera House competition: one storey has been removed, overall floor space has been reduced and views over Cardiff Bay have opened up.

An application for National Lottery funding could be another hurdle for Hadid to negotiate. Funding from the National Lottery may be limited if there is some sort of public consensus about the design. Cardiff Bay Business Forum called it a 'deconstructed pigsty' and fear of the unknown has settled on the people of Cardiff and Wales. Even Zaha Hadid was shocked, 'I never expected to be allowed to build anything in England, far less Wales'.

The Trust's target is to complete construction in time for the Opera House to open in the year 2000, reflecting the nature of the project as the ideal way for Wales and its capital city to celebrate the millennium.

The new home for the Opera House will overlook the freshwater lake which is currently under construction. The overall geometry of the 1,800- seat auditorium is perspectival (radial) rather than rectilinear to optimise viewing and to give a sense of community in an audience 'surrounding' the stage. A slight asymmetry in the geometry as well as the very different treatment of balconies on the two sides of the auditorium make the space lively and create a variety of places within the space.

The administration wing uses trusses in its four-storey high, longitudinal facades to allow an end cantilever and a central free span. These trusses are made of steel to allow as much light in as possible, and are supported on the main cores. The various cantilevering 'jewels' are supported by their flank walls which extend back into the wings, and which are anchored, either by a system of longitudinal trusses which are tied down to the ground, or by continuing down to the ground themselves.

The design offers the degree of flexibility necessary for long-term change and development. Zaha Hadid and the Trust can now look forward to the next stage of development and work towards a successful presentation to the Millennium Commission. During this stage there are likely to be further significant changes in the appearance of the building.

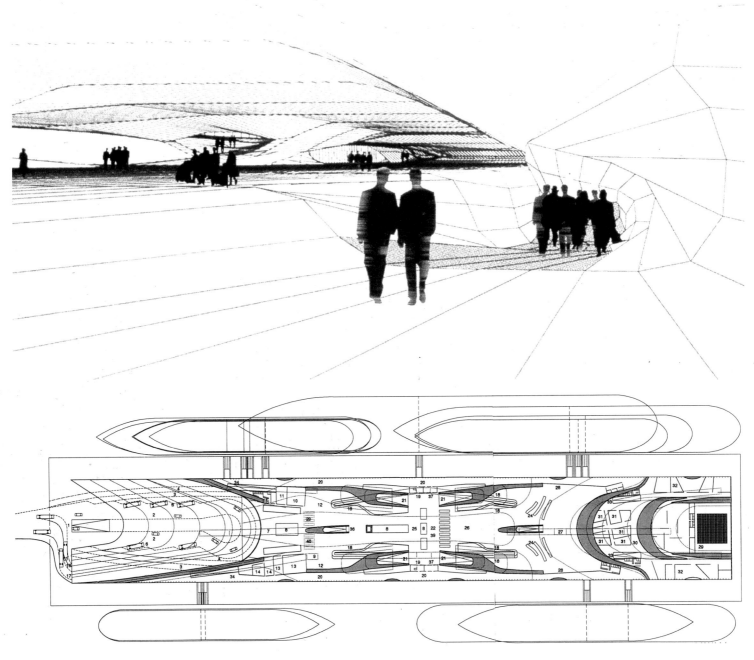

FOREIGN OFFICE ARCHITECTS
YOKOHAMA INTERNATIONAL PORT TERMINAL
Japan

Ni-wa-minato: a differential mediation

The proposed scheme aims for an artifactual rather than a representational mediation between the two components of the suggested concept of Ni-wa-minato: the *local* city of Yokohama and the *global* Pacific cruise-liner network. It will operate as a mediating device involving the two large social machines that the new institution includes: Yokohama City Waterfront and the organisation of the cruise passenger flows. Both components of the programmes are used as devices for reciprocal *de-territorialisations*: a public space that wraps around the terminal, neglecting its symbolic presence as a gate, decodifying the *rite of passage*, and a functional structure that becomes the cast of an a-typological public space, a *landscape* without instructions for occupation, rather than a *place*.

The aim is to produce a mediation of a differential nature; a machine of integration that allows us to move imperceptibly through different states into degrees of intensity, diminishing the importance of the rigid segmentation that social machines – especially those dedicated to the maintenance of borders – usually produce. The proposed artifact will minimise the energy required to change state, articulating in a differential mode the various segments of the programme through a continuous variation of form: from local citizens to the foreign visitor, from *flaneur* to business traveller, from voyeur to exhibitionist, from performer to spectator.

The scheme will produce the first perpendicular penetration of the urban space within the bay: a complementary public space to Yamashita Park using the ground surface as a device. The level of the urban ground will be connected smoothly to the boarding level, and from there will bifurcate to produce a multiplicity of urban events. The volume of the building becomes consequently an extension of the ground level of the city.

No return: The system of circulation of the building has been organised as a series of circulation loops where the programme is organised to remove borders between the dynamic and static. The construction of this multiplicity of alternative paths and bifurcations will magnify the intensity of walking through the building by duplicating the number of events encountered.

Solenoid: The plaza/terminal will not only be of a conductive nature; its function will involve the construction of a field of urban intensity through the enforcement of multiple paths and directions. In the Osanbashi Plaza, the aim is to produce a solenoid – an inductive organisation of flows – to project urban intensity inside the bay.

Weaving: The citizens and the passengers are woven through the enforcement of connections between their respective circulatory systems. The relative position of the terminal facilities and the equipment for urban leisure is reversed to increase the interaction between the two systems.

Battlefield: There will be a constant change in the volume of space required by the domestic and the international facilities due to variance in the sizes and schedules of the carriers. This will necessitate a structure which permits boundaries between domestic and international to be shifted to allow for variation in each of the areas provided. This demand for flexibility has not led us to the utmost neutral space, but to a highly differentiated structure, a continuous milieu that allows for the broadest variety of possible scenarios: an ideal battlefield, where the strategic position of a small number of elements will substantially affect the definition of the frontier. Mobile or collapsible physical barriers or surveillance points will enable the reconfiguration of the borders between territories, allowing the terminal to be 'taken' by locals, or become occupied by foreigners.

Origami: The surface of the ground folds on to itself, creating creases that not only produce and contain the paths through the building creating the differential conditions for the programme, but also provide structural strength. The traditional separation between the envelope and the load bearing structure disappears. Identification of segmented material elements such as columns, walls or floors has been avoided, to move into a materiality where differentiation between structural stresses is not determined by coded elements but rather singularities within a material continuum.

Mille-Feuille: To provide the flexibility and lightness ideal for resisting earthquake stresses, the construction will be executed entirely in steel. This extends the concept of accumulating layers, structural layers, programmatic layers, finishes . . .

This scheme by Alejandro Zaera Polo and Ms Farshid Moussavi of Foreign Office Architects was chosen from 660 entries as prize winner of Yokohama's International Port Terminal Competition

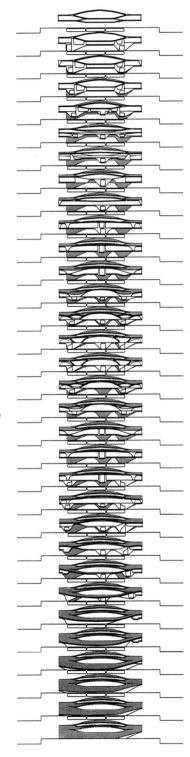

OPPOSITE, FROM ABOVE: Computer generated images of Osanbashi Plaza and Cruise Terminal; plan of Cruise Terminal; ABOVE: Transversal sections

How Buildings Learn, What Happens After They're Built Stewart Brand, Viking, 243pp, b/w ills, HB £18.00

The object of this book is to examine buildings as a whole, not just in space but in time, for buildings suffer from the forces of technology, money and fashion. The last, the author states, is change for its own sake: 'a constant unbalancing of the status quo, cruellest perhaps to buildings, which would prefer to remain just as they are.' Throughout the book, a good selection of case studies, comparative photographs and illustrations over time are used to contrast different kinds of change, drawing on commercial, domestic and institutional buildings.

The method of obtaining work through the award system is denigrated in the chapter on 'Magazine Architecture' for being based on photographs. 'Not use. Not context. Just purely visual photographs taken before people start using the building.' Back in 1929, Van Doesburg, with capitalist compulsion, warned against photographic trickery in an article for *Het Bouwbedrijf*: 'In evaluating designs, models and realised projects as shown in [Soviet] periodicals such as SA etc . . . one should be aware of technical and architectural flaws which can easily be disguised . . . In France this kind of modern photography is called photogénique. It has already caused a great deal of confusion in modern architectural production'.

The author's crusade allows him to draw on historical and contemporary examples and the experience of architects, clients, builders, and users to indicate ways in which architecture can work with time rather than against it. Last year architect Cedric Price lectured on buildings and time, emphasising the need for architects to take more interest and responsibility for their buildings after they were seen as 'complete'. Brand sees a race for finality evident in the profession, in contrast to landscape architecture where potential growth must be envisioned and planned for. On the subject of technology he states: 'Let the technology adapt to the building rather than vice versa, and then you're not pushed around when the *next* technology comes along.'

Climate Register Peter Salter and Peter Smithson, Architectural Association, 60pp, b/w ills, PB £12.00

This publication and companion volume *Imprint of India* by Alison Smithson, coincided with an exhibition held at the AA in London. The first uses the notion of 'climate register' to uncover particular environmental resonances and qualities of space and place. Focusing on four projects by Peter and Alison Smithson: the Economist Building, London; Second Arts Building, Bath; Kuwait Mat-Building, and Alexandrina Library, it emphasises the importance of understanding architecture in its specific contextual circumstances and the weathering and ageing effects on a building. Short texts, observations and illustrative material are used throughout and instructive case studies, such as the contrasting condition of the north and south facades of the AA Diploma Unit Six, Campo S. Basegio, Venice; the layered landscape and buildings of the Eastern Cemetery, Malmö, and the Macdonald and Salter Retreat Settlement on Iona where 'all-weather' accommodation is provided by a basic enclosure of steel portal frame structures clad with an aluminium corrugated skin. *Imprint of India*, a 'climate primer' was written over a period of time from 1962-1978. Its evocative vignettes complement *Climate Register*.

Earth to Spirit, In Search of Natural Architecture David Pearson, Gaia Books Ltd, 159pp, col ills, PB £11.99

Structures of apparent simplicity have frequently been overlooked. In *Shelter in Africa*, Barry Biermann wrote: 'Assessed by contemporary standards of excellence in architecture, considered as absolutes and not relative to any preconceptions, the Zulu hut stands in the forefront of architectural efficiency, constructional economy and exploitation of the nature of the material [. . . It] has achieved more in its own right than the latest advances of contemporary architecture. Any human endeavour, no matter how humble, that has attained perfection in its own field, is a rare enough phenomenon to merit due acclaim.'

Earth to Spirit evolved from a personal odyssey in search of buildings that are in harmony with nature. It introduces environmental and holistic issues involved with a new, 'gentle' architecture: which in the spirit of ancient tradition is more in tune with the natural forces and the local ecosystem. Many architects and designers across the globe are referring to ancient archetypes for direction and inspiration, and Pearson draws together connections that have emerged, recalling traditional dwellings such as the *yurt* and *tipi*.

Included in the book is Arthur Dyson's Lencioni Residence, viewed as an interactive membrane between the dynamic forces seeking expression from within and those from outside. Bart Prince's Price Residence is featured with its overhanging, biomorphic roof, as well as the inspirational organic designs by Imre Makovecz. His Roman Catholic church in Paks, Hungary possesses a fluidity of form and space that is uplifting externally and internally. Powerful carved images of angels soar above the altar, a link between earth and spirit. Influential in the creation of a stimulating environment was Rudolf Steiner, the founder of anthroposophy. He believed deeply in the effect of form on behaviour. This is inherent in Erik Asmussen's work at Järna and in the design and harmonious play of elements at the ING Bank headquarters, Amsterdam, by Ton Alberts and M van Hut. Pearson also draws attention to the vernacular examples of architects in developing countries such as Charles Correa and Hassan Fathy, and their research into the buildings of earlier civilisations, which has had a profound impact on their architecture and on the work of others.

Cities, Then and Now Jim Antoniou, Cassell, 144pp, colour ills, HB £15.99

This book looks at the history and development of eighteen cities across the globe, highlighting the effects of urbanisation on cities such as Hong Kong, Tokyo, London, Paris and New York, as well as the preventative measures taken by cities striving to retain their identity, such as Florence, Prague and Jerusalem. Relatively new cities are examined, such as San Francisco where the design has attempted to formulate modern

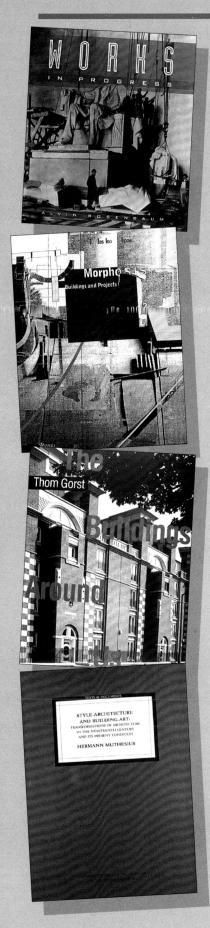

needs. Each concise focus on the cities' development and demographic change is accompanied by maps, drawings and photographs. An encouraging feature of this book for younger readers is the use of transparent overlays of key historical sites superimposed over recent photographs. Revealing aspects and features which are still in existence, the overlays communicate with immediacy the transformations of the original cityscape and make clear its contemporary condition.

Works in Progress Alvin Rosenbaum, Pomegranate Artbooks, 203pp, b/w ills, HB $39.95

Although construction photography has existed for the last 150 years, the development of many significant monuments was not always recorded visually; photographic records are not only interesting historically but useful for restoration purposes. Architectural photography often captures only the finished structure, although recording the construction process itself can help communicate more about the way a building works, especially in an age when we are confronted with increasing technological innovation. This book offers fascinating visual documentation of over eighty structures whose finished forms are worldwide landmarks. It reveals the huge construction sites that existed for large public works and buildings which often took years to complete: Brooklyn Bridge with no traffic; the Statue of Liberty in scaffolding from the waist-down; the organic towers of Gaudi's Sagrada Familia constrained by construction; the Trans-Siberian Railroad; the Titanic before her maiden voyage in 1912; the development of the Golden Gate Bridge; a prototype column of the Johnson Wax Administration showing the use of sand bags to prove its load-bearing capabilities; the Nazi Party Headquarters; TWA Terminal which Saarinen desired to express an 'upward-soaring quality of line'; the Channel Tunnel; space shuttle *Endeavour* and many other key works, each accompanied by concise descriptive text. Spanning the 1860s to the present, the book provides an evocative insight into constructional activity and the progress of form.

MORPHOSIS, Building and Projects, 1989-1992 introduced by Richard Weinstein, Rizzoli, 288pp, col ills, PB £29.95

Thom Mayne, the leading figure in Morphosis and author of the preface maintains that change, flux and contradiction are vital to Morphosis' design processes. This is not necessarily recommended for a book, where irregular typeface and images that do not correspond may force the reader to concentrate so fiercely that the contents can go largely unnoticed. What you do notice is beautifully produced images on the special vellum pages and gatefolds.

Morphosis is argumentative and comparative, accusing modern architecture of banality, repetition and meaninglessness. It applauds the dissolution of boundaries, the kinetic potential between objects, and intuitive relationships between work and culture. The practice advocates free associations and fragmentation; a drawing or model can produce a fragment which may supply the germination for a new project or take over the existing project completely. Overlap of project descriptions and images mirrors Morphosis's ongoing methodological strategy.

The book, like the architecture, seeks to unnerve and disconnect whilst introducing you to new ways of thinking about architecture – as sculpture and truth, as opposed to pragmatism and deceit.

The Buildings Around Us by Thom Gorst, E & FN Spon, 181pp, b/w ills, PB 14.95

Although equipped with an art history degree, Gorst explains the frustration he felt at not being able to understand the mix of buildings that formed the environment around him. Thus he set out to examine how ordinary buildings came to be the way they are and what they communicate to us about economic and social structures at the time of their inception. This is made clear by comparison and observation of a wide range of buildings. Constructive cross-references and explanations of key points, materials, and styles are used throughout the book. This furthers its appeal: not only are the parameters of 'architecture' extended for someone familiar with the subject, but no prior knowledge of architectural history is required.

Style-Architecture and Building Art: Transformations of Architecture in the Nineteenth Century and its Present Condition by Hermann Muthesius, The Getty Centre for the History of Art and the Humanities,132pp, b/w ills, HB $29.95, PB $19.95.

First published in 1902 Muthesius' *Stilarchitektur und Baukunst* represents one of the most important appraisals of nineteenth-century architecture and calls for a 'new' building art at the turn of the century. Trained as an architect in Berlin, Muthesius was appointed cultural and technical attaché to the German Embassy in London in 1896 – probably his best known book is the third of his studies on Contemporary English Architecture, *Das englische Haus* – and the influence of the English theorists Pugin, Ruskin, Scott and William Morris is evident throughout. In the Arts and Crafts tradition (there is an epilogue by William Morris) Muthesius believed that the new style should have its roots in the middle classes and in a tradition of domestic architecture as embodied by the work of Norman Shaw in England.

But where the invective of the English critics was waged in the Battle of Styles, in the advocation of the Gothic, Muthesius was adamant that 'the true values in building-art are totally independent of the question of style . . . a proper approach to a work of architecture has absolutely nothing to do with "style".' Here he was in tune with James Fergusson. Standing at the dawn of Modernism both men, influenced by the moral and social implications which had been injected into architecture, believed that the 'artistic authenticity' of architecture 'resides in the full correspondence of essence and form'. The root of a new architecture lay not in historical styles but the assimilation of new materials – iron and glass – and new methods of construction. Though to lift this in people's minds from the realms of engineering and utilitarian structures Muthesius recognised that a new system of aesthetics would need to evolve: 'it is a well known phenomena that artistic innovations will at first be rejected by most people . . . because popular judgements in art are almost exclusively derived from habit'.

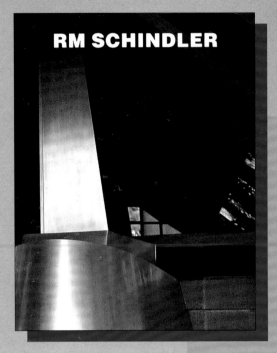

Now available in paperback, this comprehensive documentation offers a critical overview and a fresh reappraisal of Schindler's thought and works. The life and works of RM Schindler lie close to the heart of the history of early 20th-century architecture. He was a contemporary of Le Corbusier, one-time employee of Frank Lloyd Wright, and a student of Adolf Loos and Otto Wagner in Vienna. Schindler was an individualist and an innovator, influenced by his teachers, particularly Loos, but developed in America his own wholly distinctive approach, paralleling the advances of the Modern Movement and often transcending the limitations of the International Style. His original conception of Space Architecture, expounded in his writings and applied in his works, is a classic expression of modern architectural thought. With his proportional system, the Space Reference Frame, and the more concrete and pragmatic design and building techniques of the Schindler Frame, his Space Architecture provides a coherent and disciplined approach to design. The Lovell Beach House has long been acknowledged as one of a half dozen key early American modernist buildings. A wide selection of Schindler's own writings is incorporated, including a new translation of his manifesto of 1913.

NEW EDITION
Paperback 1 85490 423 X
305 x 252 mm, 264 pages
Over 345 illustrations
Publication: May 1995

Professor Reyner Banham, the leading architectural historian and critic, presents a comprehensive review of the work of architect Ron Herron, a founder member of Archigram, who tragically died in October 1994. Archigram became the most influential force in leading edge architectural design and Ron Herron probed the conventional notions of architecture and its relationship with technology and the way we live and work. Illustrated with drawings from Ron Herron's notebooks, the sketches represent both real projects and records of things seen. Also contained are details of new projects by Herron Associates including the world-famous Imagination building in London; Daimon, Kosugi and Kurobe, three projects in Japan; and the competition for the library at the British Museum, London.

Paperback 1 85490 268 7
305 x 252 mm, 128 pages
Over 200 illustrations
Publication: May 1995

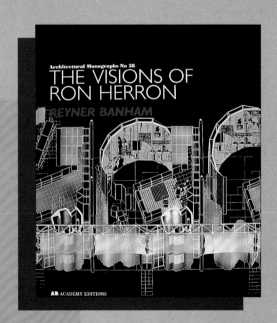

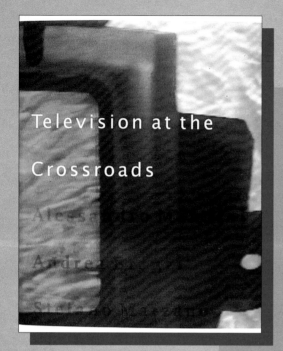

Television at the Crossroads

Where is television heading? Where will we, as viewers be following it? With technologies merging to create new multimedia possibilities and the information superhighway coming ever closer, television is about to embark on an exciting new phase in its history, one in which it will affect our lives even more deeply than it has already. Based on an innovative series of design workshops held in Italy and Holland, this book presents a collection of essays and design concepts which address precisely these issues. Eight essays focus on different aspects of television, assessing the medium's past and present, and speculating on what is to come. Sixteen original designs, interspersed throughout the book, offer ideas of what the next-but-one generation of television may look like, what its role in the home may be, and what benefits we may expect it to bring.

Hardback 1 85490 425 6
320 x 270 mm, 160 pages
180 colour illustrations and drawings
Publication: April 1995

This informative book examines the genre of portable, transportable, demountable and temporary buildings. It looks at the development of these buildings from pre-historic and traditional models through to the innovations of the classical, medieval, and Renaissance periods. Finally it examines the energetic technology transfer of the industrial Revolution. It compares the current commercially available products with the work of innovative designers such as Nicholas Grimshaw, Richard Hordern, Jan Kaplicky, and Renzo Piano and examines the philosophical and technological issues raised by their work and other more experimental and futuristic prototypes.

Paperback 1 85490 395 0
279 x 217 mm, 144 pages
180 illustrations, 35 in colour
Publication: June 1994

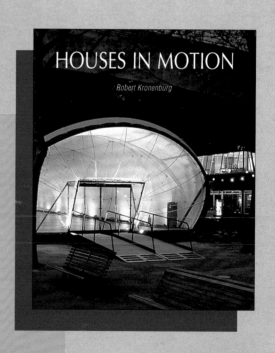

HOUSES IN MOTION
Robert Kronenburg

Further information can be obtained from Academy Group Ltd. Tel: 0171 402 2141 Fax: 0171 723 9540

SKETCHES BY EDWIN LUTYENS

Unknown to Andrew Butler and Christopher Hussey when they jointly prepared the text and illustrations for the *Lutyens Memorial* volumes in the late 1940s, were drawings tucked into the rolls of 80,000 drawings from the Lutyens office in Mansfield Street, given to the Royal Institute of British Architects by Robert Lutyens in 1951. It was Butler who volunteered to sort through the rolls in December 1951, and, in doing so, not only discovered the Lutyens schemes which were never built – the lost 'buildings on paper' – but also found several hundred original Lutyens sketches and designs, which showed him, as Butler said, to be 'an almost unrivalled artist in rough, sketch designs and sketch perspectives . . . heaps are just like things in the Uffizi!' Butler worried that he and Hussey should have known about their existence before they began work on their respective volumes, as neither had ever seen the majority of the unexecuted schemes. In *The Architecture of Sir Edwin Lutyens*, Butler had focused objectively on built work, with the exception of Liverpool Cathedral, but felt that Hussey's interpretation of Lutyens' architecture in his biography, *The Life*, might have been a little different if he had known of the brilliant sketches for so many imaginative and complex architectural ideas.

In addition, there were three other important collections of drawings which were unknown to Butler and Hussey in the late 1940s. The builder, RA Wood of JW Faulkner Ltd, rescued four early Lutyens sketchbooks from a dustbin in 1939 when the Lutyens office moved from No 5 Eaton Gate to No 13 Mansfield Street. Then Robert Lutyens gave a small group of his father's earliest designs, including those made at the South Kensington Schol of Art to his partner, Harold Grenwood, in 1953. Greenwood had been devoted to Lutyens and had done much to keep the office going in the 1930s; after his death Mrs Greenwood sold them to the RIBA, together with one hundred and thirty-four early sketches for Liverpool Cathedral, which Greenwood had preserved. Finally a group of early sketches for different schemes and a virtually complete set of working drawings for Liverpool Cathedral were found to be in George Stewart's collection, which was acquired by the RIBA in 1980. He had been with Lutyens from 1911 to the end and had later drawn the illustrations for the *Memorial* volumes.

Lutyens, like Robert Adam and Le Corbusier, had a gift for drawing and painting that went beyond architecture. But unlike Adam and Le Corbusier, who channelled their creative energies into Picturesque landscapes or Cubist paintings, Lutyens rarely sketched buildings or landscapes in a topographical sense or produced paintings as works of art. He drew constantly, however, illustrating letters in a spontaneous and pictorial way with doodles and figures, plans and ideas. He also produced 'vivreations', Lutyens' word for all light-hearted activities, in the form of drawings to amuse his children, friends and clients. This gift meant that he was able, from an early age, to realise his concepts on paper and to see 'in the round'. For Lutyens would rarely talk about architecture although his visual memory was phenomenal; he knew St Paul's by heart and absorbed what he wanted from buildings in the past without feeling the need to sketch them. He could also draw from dictation. Hussey describes the episode when he drew up the designs which were dictated by an old, blind Sapper and how he later recommended this exercise to the Cambridge Architectural Society in 1932.

In spite of this, Lutyens doubted his own draughtsmanship, particularly in his early years, just as he regretted his lack of a public school education. When his wife, Lady Emily, reported in 1900 that Lord Battersea, Lutyens' client for The Pleasaunce at Overstrand, had said that he was 'the finest draughtsman he had ever seen', Lutyens replied, 'What rot Lord B saying that about my draughtsmanship. I don't like it!! It is so insincere and untrue.'

'Sketches by Edwin Lutyens' is at the RIBA, London from 27th April until 1st July 1995. This excerpt is from the companion book by Margaret Richardson, curator of the exhibition, published by Academy Editions.

ABOVE: Preliminary design for Munstead, Surrey, from the Munstead Wood sketchbook, c1893; BELOW: Record sketch of the design for the Memorial to the Missing at St Quentin, Nord, France, c1923

BRITISH ARCHITECTS IN EXILE

IAN RITCHIE, COMPUTER-GENERATED IMAGE, GLASBLAU SEELE FACTORY, GERMANY

Architectural Design

BRITISH ARCHITECTS IN EXILE

KLEIN DYTHAM, TOKYO FRONTIER, EXPO '96, JAPAN; *OPPOSITE*: SIR NORMAN FOSTER, LYCÉE POLYVALENT, FRÉJUS

ACADEMY EDITIONS • LONDON

Acknowledgements

All material is courtesy of the authors and architects unless otherwise stated.
The Exile of Ralph Erskine: Box, Barge and Ark is published with acknowledgements to Peter Collymore, *The Architecture of Ralph Erskine*, Academy Editions, London, 1994. The computer-generated image *p46 above,* The Glasblau Seele Factory, was designed in conjunction with Ove Arup and Partners; *p46 below,* Terrasson – Continent de l'imaginaire was developed with Kathryn Gustafson of Paysage Land, Arc Ingénierie and Ove Arup and Partners. The computer-generated image *p48 above,* the glass hall for the Messe in Leipzig was developed in conjunction with GMP Architects (Professor Marg, Herr Polonyi and HL-Technik); image *p48, below* the designs for the new headquarters for MERO, was developed by ARUP GmbH, Berlin. The Kumamoto Grasslands Agricultural Institute *pp56-57* was designed in conjunction with Inga Dagfinnsdottir and Ojukai Furukawa Architects. The Toyama Observation Platform *pp58-59* was designed with Inaba-Miyoi Architects. The Wiesbaden House *pp72-75* was the result of a competition initiated and organised by Fritz Küstner of Galerie zB. The Nara Convention Centre *pp92-94* was designed in conjunction with Andrew Yeoman and John Kramer.

Front Cover: Cook and Hawley, Office Development, Hamburg
Inside Covers: Studio Granda, Reykjavik City Hall, Iceland

Photographic Credits
All material is courtesy of the authors and architects unless otherwise stated.
Dennis Gilbert *pp2, 38-39, 76-81*; Tomio Ohashi *p3*; Norbert Miguletz *pp6, 76-81*; Tim Soar *p13;* Alan Williams *p34 above;* Peter Collymore *pp34 below, 35;* Paul Raftery *p36*; Richard Bryant/Arcaid *pp40-45*; Christian Richters *pp50, 52-55*; Guy Pollock *pp64-65*; Kabushisa Kida *pp66-69*; Charlie Stebbings *p82*; Chas Wilder *pp88-90*; Andy Keate *p92*; Nacasa & Partners *p94*; Koji Horiuchi *p95*

EDITOR: Maggie Toy
EDITORIAL TEAM: Iona Spens (Senior Editor), Stephen Watt
ART EDITOR: Andrea Bettella CHIEF DESIGNER: Mario Bettella DESIGNER: Phil Kirwin

CONSULTANTS: Catherine Cooke, Terry Farrell, Kenneth Frampton, Charles Jencks, Heinrich Klotz, Leon Krier, Robert Maxwell, Demetri Porphyrios, Kenneth Powell, Colin Rowe, Derek Walker

First published in Great Britain in 1995 by *Architectural Design* an imprint of
ACADEMY GROUP LTD, 42 LEINSTER GARDENS, LONDON W2 3AN
Member of the VCH Publishing Group
ISBN: 1 85490 249 0 (UK)

Distributed to the trade in the United States of America by
ST MARTIN'S PRESS, 175 FIFTH AVENUE, NEW YORK, NY 10010

Printed and bound in Italy

Contents

EDITORIAL
Maggie Toy

Embedded in the notion of exile are the implications of hostility, of rejection and dissatisfaction. Devoting an issue exclusively to the subject runs the risk of appearing to express a biased and insupportable grudge blinded from reason. This presentation should be understood as an attempt to highlight a worrying trend which forces talent away from the United Kingdom in order for creative potential to be both realised and recognised. At the same time, research also reveals, as we have presented, that many architects deny that such a problem exists and think that quibbling about such petty difficulties may be a waste of time.

Such as it may be, the problem is real enough for debates to be held questioning the direction of architecture's future in Britain. Are similar debates being staged world-wide? Are the concerns confined strictly to this country? Does every country pine for the missed architectural opportunities?

For a variety of contributory factors, much architecture in Britain has been retrogressive and often stifling for the wealth of talented designers working within this country. Currently the debate continues over the best way to exploit the potential fortune of the Millennium Fund. How can this contribute to encouraging a positive view of the built environment?

The political strength that enabled the building of landmarks such as the Sydney Opera House or the Eiffel Tower will not be recreated here at the present time, as clearly pointed out by Jonathan Glancey. But is it not possible to create the same kind of awareness of the built environment as that prevailing in France, for example, where the *Grand Projets* herald a forward thinking electorate?

However, to be of the mind that every other country has a better system is not necessarily the justified; looking towards other European examples does not always lead to optimism. Berlin is undergoing a huge change of face and yet, whilst many opportunities are open to foreign architects, it is also argued that such a strong grip is held over all planning restrictions that only a few favoured architects are succeeding and others – perhaps they too are facing exile.

Despite all this, the collection of architectural works presented here serves also to celebrate that which is good design, evidence of a wealth of talent primarily based in Britain and despite this location finding the opportunity to build.

The notion of exile is discussed by Michael Spens who identifies a specifically English problem, whilst Kenneth Powell celebrates the English High Tech; Norman Foster not only builds prolifically abroad but also remains the popular choice within his own country. The 'bizarre' architecture of Peter Cook is being built abroad and yet to many UK residents, it seems, is frequently considered interesting but unbuildable. We also look back to exiles of a previous generation, such as Ralph Erskine, who in spite of spending most of his architectural career in Scandinavia has now donated 'The Ark' to the London skyline. From this 'old master exile' we run through the chronological gamut, taking in Ian Ritchie who enjoys residing in London but usually executes his innovative designs abroad, and younger practices such as Studio Granda and Ushida Findlay who are learning to expand their horizons in order to build.

There frequently appears to be a lack of encouragement towards young talent, in fact on some occasions a positive discouragement; some world renowned figures openly stating that it would be beneficial for students to travel and gain experience before returning. Whilst there is something distinctly healthy about this point of view it is also potentially very dangerous: a system which encourages talent to leave the fold surely provides little for its return? So what may appear to be a strengthening, growing experience for young architects may also lead to a dire lack of innovative architectural discourse within Britain.

But there are many reasons for optimism and hope. I am delighted to see that the innovative designs of Future Systems are being built, perhaps this might be the indication of a brighter architectural future. Surely, until we are able to demonstrate to the public at large how wonderful the experience of space can be within 'modern' buildings it is going to be impossible to not only assist people in developing a more comprehensive view of what their built environment could be like, but to offer a whole and free decision and a real choice. Perhaps, then, the instinct for the experiment would be able to return to a presently rocky British architectural scene.

Studio Granda, Aktion Poliphile – house in Wiesbaden, Germany

MICHAEL SPENS
BRITISH ARCHITECTS IN EXILE

Exile is a practice or a set of practices. To the underprivileged, home is represented not by a house but by a practice or a set of practices. Everyone has his own. These practices, chosen and not imposed, offer in their repetition, transient as they may be in themselves, more permanence, more shelter than any lodging.
John Berger

John Berger was dealing with the state of exile, away from homelands, but his definition is not inappropriate to architects. Exile was a particular product of the 1980s climate for architecture in England (and I mean England, rather than other parts of the United Kingdom, where regional architecture of generalised mediocrity was sustained by the uninspired clientele that exercised executive power), whereby the category of the 'new' was extended to include an array of Post-Modernist games that today look distinctly flyblown where they stand.

At the same time there developed a growing appreciation abroad of the ability of a handful of architects, pathfinders of necessity. The American groves of Academe, especially the Ivy League and the East Coast, were diverted by the burgeoning talents of James Stirling and the related teaching skills of Colin St John Wilson and Colin Rowe: for a golden moment they were teaching over here, but soon building and, or, teaching over there. Archigram won the Monte Carlo Competition in the early 70s, and it seemed the next generation was poised to take-off. With the Pompidou Centre it did, and in the Pacific Rim, Norman Foster built the finest, most elegant tower for a bank anywhere – in Hong Kong.

By the mid-80s, key architects of the younger 'taught' generation were themselves on the catapult ready for take-off. They all taught increasingly in Germany and entered more and more competitions, whether open or by invitation across Europe. Partly this was in the absence of a credible competition culture in Britain. What competitions there were became tampered or meddled with in a classically subversive, proprietorial English way, from the top down. It was sickening to know that propriety did not really exist, that hidden agendas prevailed, and anachronisms flourished under the guise of eccentricity, English-style. We had Norman Wisdom, kind hearts, coronets and architects. Occasionally, like Poulson, they slipped up, or, precursors of the 1980s, were grabbed by greed.

Exile is not only a set of practices, but the escape from malpractice, the search for new horizons. It has to be remembered that the prophets who spread to the UK and Europe were first the teachers. To those mentioned above could be added Alan Colquhoun and Robert Maxwell, and more latterly Lionel March. Whilst in Germany Peter Cook blazed a trail from Frankfurt. These activities prepared the ground for broader acceptance of the exceptionally highly skilled product of key British schools of the 1960s and 70s. From the historic win of the Centre Pompidou by Rogers and Piano, there followed at last the Lloyds building in the City of London. This after the demise of the Spence and Webster masterpiece which won the House of Commons additions competition (but was duly abandoned). By the 1980s Stirling was building seriously in Stuttgart, and had been awarded the Turner Wing at the Tate in belated recognition, close to the time when the Cambridge History Library was saved from demolition. Foster's success with the Sainsbury Centre had led to the Nîmes commission.

The voluntary practice of exile, so neatly defined by Berger above, develops its own transient patterns and codes of thinking and doing, allowing new senses of security. So it is true in architecture. The habit of circulating and meeting commissions abroad renders the practitioners more at home that 'at home'. What of those practices who paradoxically had a break on their home ground in those lucky days of anything goes Thatcherism? Michael Hopkins has felt no need to hunt abroad. Farrell likewise has mastered a variant of the Post-Modern which complies with British ideas of the acceptably modern.

After the mid-80s, for some, the pattern set in. Certainly for James Stirling, it was genuinely easier to work in Europe, the technology there, especially in Germany, came to suit his method of design. Until then, exile was not a widespread condition. We could be flattered to feel that Eva Jiricna and Jan Kaplicky were still with us, seemingly preferring the culture since 1986.

Cook and Hawley, Stadelschule Kantine, Frankfurt

Temporary adventures meant escape from the high tide of the enterprise culture. But princely concern about, and suspicion of the new, combined with this brittle atmosphere to destabilise modernism, rendering it thus locally suspect, swathing institutional and 'Hello' taste alike in a *gemütlichkeit* of the coy reference, the ironic built-aside design (such as Grand Buildings, Trafalgar Square and their opposite neighbour uphill, the National Gallery extension, more Post Office than even Post-Modern). All this was duly to be assuaged with a ponderous, bogus contextuality. Trafalgar Square, by 1989, combined the remembrance of times past with a tear-jerking Royal Architectural Tournament of unspeakable banality. So we have it, for some generations to come.

As the 1980s proceeded, new highlights occurred: Alsop won the open competition (157 entries) for the headquarters and government centre of the region of Bouches-du-Rhône, in Marseilles. A new generation that had grown-up on competitions was flexing its muscles to take over. Alsop still has little to show in this country. The National Centre for Literature, won by Alsop in 1993, has like a mirage, been subverted by atmospheric forces and disappeared: just as Zaha Hadid's Cardiff Opera House win almost disappeared in a puff of blue smoke. In this country, to win a competition doesn't necessarily take you anywhere but to be famous for the day (of the announcements) as Andy Warhol might say. It's a surreal world we architects inhabit, transient to a degree. Which is why it is generally easier to be transient abroad, for some of our best talents.

This is all the more remarkable in that Britain still boasts the most integrated, lively cohesive, mind-blowing and persuasive architectural culture in the world. The combined world of all that exists in this country, the schools, leading practices, press and television coverage, publishing networks and exhibitions comprising this 'world' are not exceeded by quality in any other country in terms of their collective achievement. Yet this structure, this network, exists under constant threat. The schools fight off government efforts to reduce the curriculum to four years and to diminish their essential research base in the universities. Press columns in the national papers have to be continually argued for, against cookery column demands, or sport inches. The profession remains under threat of deregulation when it effectively has been the model profession structure the world over. The ethos that lies at the basis of architectural design has to be constantly fought for, upheld, and explained to University Boards. The embryonic, now 'millennium-inspired' competition system is constantly undermined as we have seen earlier. Grandees dabble,

intervene, withdraw and leave projects, sponsorship plans and careers crippled by their indecisively amateurish play. Meanwhile the visual excitement sought by a new generation, those still at school, is provided for by the media, by electronic highways, and by CD Rom. All these are real inspirational tools which can be mobilized to turn the tide, to re-establish practices and new modes, which in turn will find creative fulfilment on home ground again.

Now too there is a curious situation to redress, best epitomized in the results of the Tate Gallery Bankside Gallery competition. The Trustees have opted for a scheme not dissimilar from those of other competitors, yet one that is distinctly middle-of-the-road. It is in no way at all reprehensible that the selected architects are from abroad. It is in fact the absolutely recognisable fruition of a catalogue of uncertainties in other directions. British culture, it is decided 'needs' stimulus from outside. The heads can be seen nodding in assent, a forest of mandarins. The media respond. Controversy has been circumvented.

A countervailing argument frequently is pursued, which goes as follows. England has seen its most talented architects fulfilled in the past 20 years – Stansted Airport, Waterloo Station, Lloyd's and the new theatre at Glynbourne all testify to this. Yet these isolated breakthroughs cannot mask a graveyard of missed opportunities. What about the National Gallery Extension, Compton Verney Opera House, Windsor Castle, the National Literature Centre and the Cardiff Bay Opera House (in Swansea) for example. It is in the operation and fulfilment of the conditions of major competitions that disaster strikes, like some kind of debilitating nervous disease. The paradox is that while all this has been going on, there has been a quiet revolution in the quality of Foreign Office building overseas – witness the new Chancery building for the British Embassy in Prague by Jesticoe and Wiles. The problem clearly lies at home, and in the commissioning products for home consumption.

Here in 1995, assuaged by the blandishments of the heritage industry, the whole question of exile resonates within a particularly British version of culture. For example, the whole question of patronage has to be looked at afresh in the special 'windfall' phenomenon of the Millennium Fund. The celebration of architecture here in England has always been ambiguous. The important and symbolic buildings of London are by European standards of their times undistinguished. St Paul's Cathedral and Buckingham Palace are important and significant punctuations in the city plan but they remain as provincial nonentities architecturally. It is vital that entry into the new century is marked by the celebration of an architecture that is of the highest order. Signs are that the commissions will include some exiles, prodigals returning to join those who remain.

It is useful in examining the background to such a condition of contemporary exile to explore the impact of new, imported cultural influences upon the grass roots of English culture in the mid-18th century. In the ascendancy that saw Burlington establish Palladianism in England, Wren and Hawksmoor had been put out to grass. The highly inventive local variant of the baroque was superseded by what can only be described as a wave of modernism, culminating in the construction of Chiswick House, a Villa Savoye or Villa Mairea of its time. Kent and later Lancelot 'Capability' Brown, followed in establishing a reconciliation of the country seats of power and patronage with the concept of 'natural' landscape. All the time, English grass roots culture ranted and raved, represented most typically by the raunchy emissions of Hogarth's pen and brush.

These tirades have persisted. Brown is to this day plagued by reactionary sentiments, themselves clothed in sweet romanticisms. 'The Tory View of Landscape' is represented by a recent publication that seeks again to put the clock back, driving another nail in Capability Brown's coffin in the process. The preconditions for architectural exile have long roots. Whereas enlightened patronage kept Kent and Brown in full employment then, if they existed in a contemporary form today, they would certainly have languished or been driven into exile. Indeed Brown's exacting professionalism would have almost certainly been undermined by a host of cost cutting imitators. The heritage industry is here. If the new patrons of the Millennium Fund are not to be sucked in, real judgment and quality will have to work together to select architects of the highest talent. The exiles must be given their chance.

We live in an area of confusion, and one where no longer do 'things' improve inevitably, as part of 'progress'. Progress seems to be over, at least in this country. The same patterns of behaviour, the practices to which Berger has so succinctly referred, will persist. The culture will not noticeably improve. The chances are, in fact, that it will deteriorate. It is fitting that an issue is devoted to 'exile'. Because there, but for the grace et cetera, go all of us.

The culture lives, in exile. Our best teachers (eg Rowe, Balfour) seemed destined to return abroad again. Alsop has taken up a chair in Vienna. Sudjic is in Holland, British architects are all over the Pacific Rim. Ron Herron was just getting there when he died. The next generation will not miss out in Ron's wake.

An enduring ambivalence traditionally characterises British patronage revealing a flawed approach to the indigenous roots and historical basis of its own culture. What intrigues foreign commentators on this culture is its persistent ability to throw up, and out, unique and original talents that help to broaden acceptable precepts of taste. This taste is invariably bad, and these new talents usually achieve an expressive formal originality no less powerful than the baroque innovations of Inigo Jones. Nigel Coates succeeds in Japan by drawing upon the same divergent impulses. Much the same could be said of Ron Herron's recent work in Malaysia, and further back, of Archigram's collective visions, and of James Stirling's sheer genius. Yet sadly our great talents are usually appreciated too little and too late. There are five years left before the millennium.

Alsop & Störmer, Kaufhaus Des Nordens, Hamburg

KENNETH POWELL
NOTIONS OF EXILE

Richard Rogers (we are told by his biographer, Brian Appleyard) was reluctant to enter the 1971 competition for the Centre Georges Pompidou in Paris. He and his then partner, Renzo Piano, had submitted an entry to the competition earlier that year for the Burrell collection in Glasgow – it sank without a trace. It was Ted Happold, then with Ove Arup, who persuaded Piano that the Paris job was worth trying for and together they convinced Rogers. In July that year, Piano and Rogers heard that they had won.

It was appropriate enough that the successful bid for the Pompidou Centre was 'engineering-led'. The scheme was a celebration of engineering, and not only of the 19th century British tradition – which influenced Rogers' Lloyd's Building even more clearly. In Paris itself, Rogers and Piano had discovered the Maison de Verre by Chareau and Bijvoet (the latter an 'exile' from Holland) and marvelled at the elegance with which mass-produced elements were used. They also knew the Maison du Peuple in Clichy (1939), ostensibly the work of the architects Beaudoun and Lods but engineered by Jean Prouvé, *le constructeur* as he liked to be known, conveniently one of the most influential members of the competition jury. Prouvé was to be, in due course, a helpful counsellor on the project, advising Piano and Rogers not to let the purity of their concept be watered down by a collaboration with a French executive practice.

A truly cosmopolitan mix of themes and influences – futurism, constructivism, Louis Kahn, Cedric Price – underlay the Pompidou scheme. The completed building is both Piano's and Roger's, but the British element in it is strong. Cedric Price and Joan Littlewood's 1965 'Fun Palace' project was certainly in the background and nobody who moved in the Architectural Association circles in the 60s could ignore Archigram.

Archigram was not just a movement but, for a few years, a practice. Its victory in the Monte Carlo casino competition could have propelled Peter Cook, Denis Crompton and Ron Herron to instant fame. But the project was cancelled, while Pompidou went ahead. The idea of the project – very Archigram inspired – as a cross between 'an information-orientated, computer-ised Times Square and the British Museum' did not entirely survive into the completed building. Pompidou, however, established Rogers on the world scene and effectively created the practice of which he remains the titular head. It was seen, at the time and for years after, as a symbol of the capacity of the British profession to break out of its insular mould, away from the remains of the old empire and into a wider world of opportunity. Architecture became a well publicised British export.

Beaubourg (as everyone called the project) was important not just in symbolic but in practical terms too as a link between Britain and the global world of practice. Peter Rice, who was brought in to work on the project by Happold, remained a close collaborator of Rogers for the rest of his life, but his association with Piano was even closer – as Rogers and Piano parted company in 1977 – eventually forming a partnership. Ian Ritchie subsequently worked extensively with Rice in France in the RFR practice, one of a number of British architects in a broadly 'High Tech' tradition to bypass Britain and achieve success on an international stage. Ritchie (ex-Foster) had previously joined up with Mike Dowd and Alan Stanton (members of Rogers' Pompidou team) to form Chrysalis. Dowd has continued to work from Paris, as has Ken Armstrong, battling with the problems of the Maison du Japon project.

Norman Foster's win in the Hong Kong and Shanghai Bank competition of 1978-79 seemed to confirm the message of Beaubourg. As a demonstration of the world-beating potential of British High Tech, indeed, the Hong Kong Bank was far more significant. Foster saw off a posse of straight (basically International Style) modernists, including Harry Seidler, Hugh Stubbins, SOM and YRM, and, amazingly, persuaded the client that a highly expressive landmark building could equally provide a unique solution to their long-term needs. Like Rogers at Lloyd's, Foster impressed with his emphasis on growth and flexibility. High Tech, indeed, seemed likely to become the new International Style. The bank required Foster to establish a new way of working globally – which opened the way to later projects in France, Spain, Germany, Japan and the USA (not to mention the ongoing new airport in Hong Kong). With a

Sir Norman Foster, Carré d'Art, Nîmes

sizeable team based in Hong Kong, the Foster office became truly international. A generation of young architects, like Alex Lifschutz and Ian Davidson, who came back to London to form Lifschutz Davidson, had a forceful – but invaluable – introduction to the world scene.

British High Tech was not, of course, an entirely home-grown product – Norman Foster's acknowledged debt to Buckminster Fuller is immense and both he and Rogers were strongly influenced by West Coast America, while Rogers' Italian roots count for more than is sometimes recognized. (Rogers' urbanistic agenda, well expressed in his recent, 1995, Reith Lectures, owes something to his memories of Florence). The movement, if such it was, was enriched by *émigrés* to Britain. The Czechs Eva Jiricna and Jan Kaplicky arrived in 1968 and subsequently worked intermittently with Foster and Rogers. Their paths diverged, Jiricna becoming know as a designer of interiors (Rogers brought her in to work on those at Lloyd's) while Kaplicky's Future Systems practice – a partnership with Amanda Levete (ex-Rogers) – continues to amaze the architectural world with its visions of a new world, governed by benign technology, which owes a good deal to those of Buckminster Fuller. Future Systems' near win in the 1989 Bibliothèque de France competition was seen, rightly or wrongly, as a set-back for Britain's architectural export programme. The French, it was feared, had decided that it was a good time to patronize local talent and Dominique Perrault got the job. The Foster/Rogers circle produced a string of successful new practices during the 1980s. If most did not make an instant impact on the international scene, the high level of activity in that decade helps to explain why. Equally, Foster and Rogers themselves played the international competition game with a fair degree of success, though neither had quite the same standing around the world of James Stirling, whose own version of British architecture was radically at odds with the High Tech. Stirling was able, for example, to build on a scale in the USA, where neither Foster or Rogers have, even now, made a major breakthrough. Foster's version of the Humana Building could not have been more different from Michael Graves' 'oversized Jukebox' – but would the American critics who lashed out at Graves have loved Foster any more. In fact, his largest American project to date is a relatively modest museum, far away from the major cities. High Tech architects have always found the diversity of the American scene confusing and depressing – Frank Gehry is rather reluctantly admired in Britain today in the way that Wright was in the 1950s: both are 'too American' for some people's tastes.

Japan has proved a fruitful field for Rogers, though the projects he has completed there so far are relatively modest in scale. Foster's Millennium Tower remains the great unbuilt High Tech monument of all. That unorthodox member of the High Tech academy (he would surely disown membership), David Chipperfield, made his reputation with Japanese projects. Chipperfield served his time in the offices of both Foster and Rogers before setting-up his own practice in 1984. He was one of the Foster Hong Kong team and moved naturally into working in Japan. As teacher and educator in a broader sense (he was one of the founders of the 9H Gallery, a focus for world architecture in the 80s) Chipperfield's reputation is immense and his own work has long moved far from its roots. His speculative scheme for rebuilding Windsor Castle after the 1992 fire was a model of rational calm. Ironically, however, Chipperfield's international reputation has not won him work in Britain – losing the recent Tate Bankside competition was a considerable disappointment after his near miss in the Berlin museum competition.

The British pavilion at the 1991 Venice architecture Biennale appeared to be a celebration of the triumph of High Tech. Though Stirling (who was to die the following year) and John Outram (whose work is so outrageously unconventional as to be acceptable) were included, the other four architects represented belonged firmly within the movement; Rogers and Foster were there, and so too were Grimshaw and Hopkins, neither of whom were quite international stars. Both, according to Richard Burdett, who wrote the catalogue of the show, were specifically British figures:

> Grimshaw's and Hopkins' architecture is suited to the dry precision of the English language and has the same fine and elegant structure, which welds an idea to its expression, shaping the shell to fit exactly the mechanics of its function.

Grimshaw has since 'broken through' onto the European scene, notably with his Seville Pavilion, Berlin Stock Exchange and Igus factory projects – which he is now in the process of extending. His Waterloo International Terminal, used by travellers from Brussels and Paris, is a wonderful showcase for his work. Hopkins, however, remains overwhelmingly a British practitioner. Like Basil Spence in the 1950s and early 60s, he has caught the national mood. Glyndebourne and the new Parliamentary Building are specifically – and quite understandably – the products of a national culture, part of an architecture which it would be hard to export. Hopkins' earlier work, exemplified by his own house and the Schlumberger complex at Cambridge is another matter

– but it took him some time to emerge fully from the shadow of Norman Foster. At present, it is hard to see how he needs foreign commissions.

Hopkins has, of course, pushed the definition of High Tech to its absolute limits to emerge as perhaps the establishment architect of the 90s in Britain, a phenomenon whose potent appeal embraces history, context and nature as well as technology (and the latter in a quiet, reflective manner which has nothing to do with the thrills of Schlumberger). None of the architects I have mentioned would confess these days to being High Tech – or to have ever been High Tech. A stock response would be to cite 'appropriate' technology. Both Foster and Rogers are anxious to stress their interest in ecology and 'green' buildings – environmental friendliness is a prominent feature of recent projects such as Rogers' Strasbourg Court of Human Rights and Foster's ongoing Frankfurt Commerzbank. Both the great masters remain extremely exportable. The cosmopolitan nature of their offices – Foster claims up to 20 nationalities amongst his colleagues – helps.

Other firms in the High Tech tradition have found the going harder. Troughton McAslan (the partners both worked on Rogers' Lloyd's) is something of a maverick on the world scene. Cooperation with Ove Arup and the route Rogers followed to win Pompidou got them St Catherine's College at Kobe, a cool, history conscious design which managed to survive the Japanese system of contracting to emerge as one of the most interesting British buildings in Japan. The same process has since won them a sizeable job in Turkey, while McAslan's special interest in refurbishing classic modern movement structures (like the De la Warr Pavilion at Bexhill-on-Sea) helped to secure a consultancy at Florida Southern College, Frank Lloyd Wright's largest work and now in need of extensive repair. A commission of this sort is probably marginal (at best) in financial terms but has helped Troughton McAslan to secure

fairly regular coverage in journals in Europe, Japan and the USA.

If there was a moment when the High Tech movement suffered a particularly momentous reverse it was the appointment of Will Alsop for the Hôtel du Département, Marseilles, in 1990. Foster had produced a strong scheme and was a hot tip for the commission – his entry, indeed, was both 'green' and highly expressive. But at a moment when the French scene seemed to be closing in, Alsop won the job which helped him to claim his place at the top table of British architects. It is nearly a decade since a major exhibition at the Royal Academy identified the 'big three' of British architecture as Foster, Rogers and Stirling. The exercise would be impossible today – and pointless – though Alsop's claim to the place Stirling vacated place is probably stronger than that of Michael Hopkins or Nicholas Grimshaw.

There is currently some talk of a 'crisis' of High Tech, even suggestions that the school which has dominated British architecture for nearly 20 years is in retreat. True, the leading practices have changed their approach – although Rogers' Channel 4 headquarters relies on many of the devices seen at Lloyd's, but they remain strong. Foster may not have the cutting edge he had in the 70s, but the rebirth of his practice as a latter-day version of SOM may not be entirely a bad thing. SOM (before it went Post-Modernist) was one of the pillars of good modern commercial architecture worldwide. Perhaps there never was a school or movement, just a lot of personal and professional connections and convenient critical label. But High Tech existed and was instrumental in helping to create a world architectural culture in the aftermath of the (so-called) International Style. In the end, it ushered in diversity and pluralism. That Zaha Hadid will – one hopes – build in Cardiff and Herzog and de Meuron at Bankside is a consequence of Foster and Rogers' internationalism.

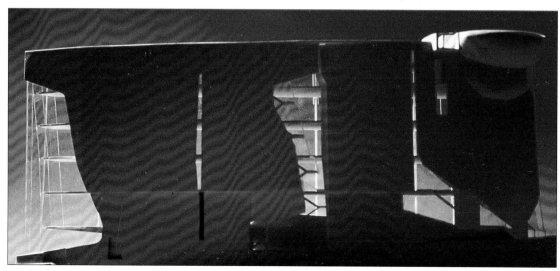

Cook and Hawley, Office Development, Hamburg

PETER COOK AND CHRISTINE HAWLEY

PROPHETS IN THEIR OWN COUNTRY
Some Questions and Answers

Since beginning (at last) to build, you and Christine Hawley still seem to be (only) doing things for foreign cities? Why do you think this is?
– The inherent conservatism in England versus the inherent fascination with progress in Japan or Germany: where even the philistines will argue against progressives in the same terms.

Why stay based in London then?
– First of all, there is a brilliant and almost anarchic character to English architectural thinking and designing that is short on keeping to the rules and constantly inventing its way out of corners. Combined with the 'boffin' tradition it is no wonder that the 'schoolboy inventor' aspect of our character has led to English 'High Tech'.

You and Christine are known as architectural academics, how does this fit with your work as designers ?
– We sometimes feel almost like an extinct species: since Michael Brawne and Andy Macmillan have retired there is almost no one running an architectural school in the UK who is also a designer. Yet in most European countries and the USA the outstanding professors all build and draw. From Louis Kahn, through Matthias Ungers to Michael Rotondi there is a creative-educative tradition that we ignore at our peril. In this country it is assumed that if you build you must be ignoring your academic 'duties' and that if you are a teacher-director that you are an amateur architect. The reality is different. I feel most confident and pertinent as a critic when I am in the middle of a good creative 'run' on the drawing board. Similarly, I sit drawing with seminar conversation running through my head as I tweak a corner or decide on a door position.

How do you feel about the context of the places you design – do you consciously try to be 'British' for instance?
– We have become increasingly familiar with Germany, where I have taught for many years, and nowadays with Japan. We consciously talk to our friends about the nuances of their cities. With regard to housing, we tend to approach the designs from the point of view of a 'story-line' even creating characters for members of the family. Whilst not being consciously British we do probably set up a 'debate' between the various buildings we have designed. One very noticeable characteristic is the 'front-to-back' thing. There is a tendency for our schemes to have a 'hard' and a 'soft' side. For instance, our Langen museum was quiet on the north and ebullient on the south, whilst the Berlin-Lutzowplatz housing is 'rational' on the east and 'voluptuous' on the west. Our Hamburg offices are cliff like on the north and sleek on the south.

What do you feel is the difference in architectural atmosphere in London compared with other places?
– In London, the world of 'thinkers' and 'doers' is much the most divided. In London, for instance, there are four main centres of 'High Tech' architecture: at the cutting edge of the world. Yet none of them permits their staff to teach (though they are eager enough to recruit bright students). On the other side, many teachers are afraid to 'soil' their position by part-time office work (assuming it was available). In Germany, the professors and assistants in the schools are all involved in offices – their own or somebody's. Some even work out of their studios on real jobs.

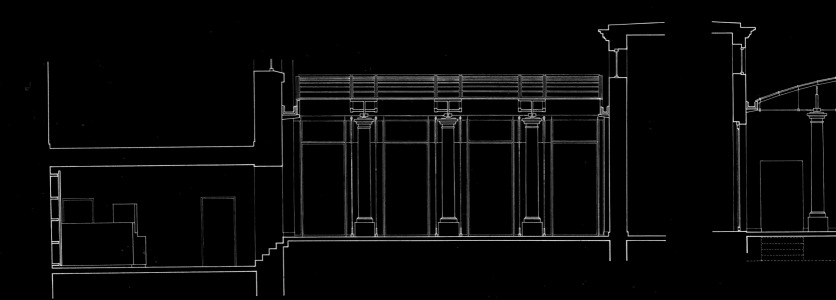

STADELSCHULE
Frankfurt

Cook and Hawley have been associated with the Stadelschule (art academy) since 1978 and know the building intimately. When commissioned to insert a canteen into an existing courtyard and some internal rooms, their aim was to retain the atmosphere of this airy building.

The result is very much due to the close coincidence of view between the two architects and Professor Bollinger – himself an exquisite designer. The principal 'trick' is to apparently just drape a glass structure over most of the pre-existing courtyard and some retained columns and then – 'hey presto' open the roof in one go when it gets warm. It has been working well and appears almost nonchalant – as was the intention.

Detailing is deliberately slim – and tough. The bar area is not yet being used as exotically as the architects intended: but may in the future.

BELOW L TO R: Longitudinal section; Cross-section

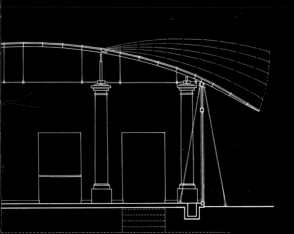

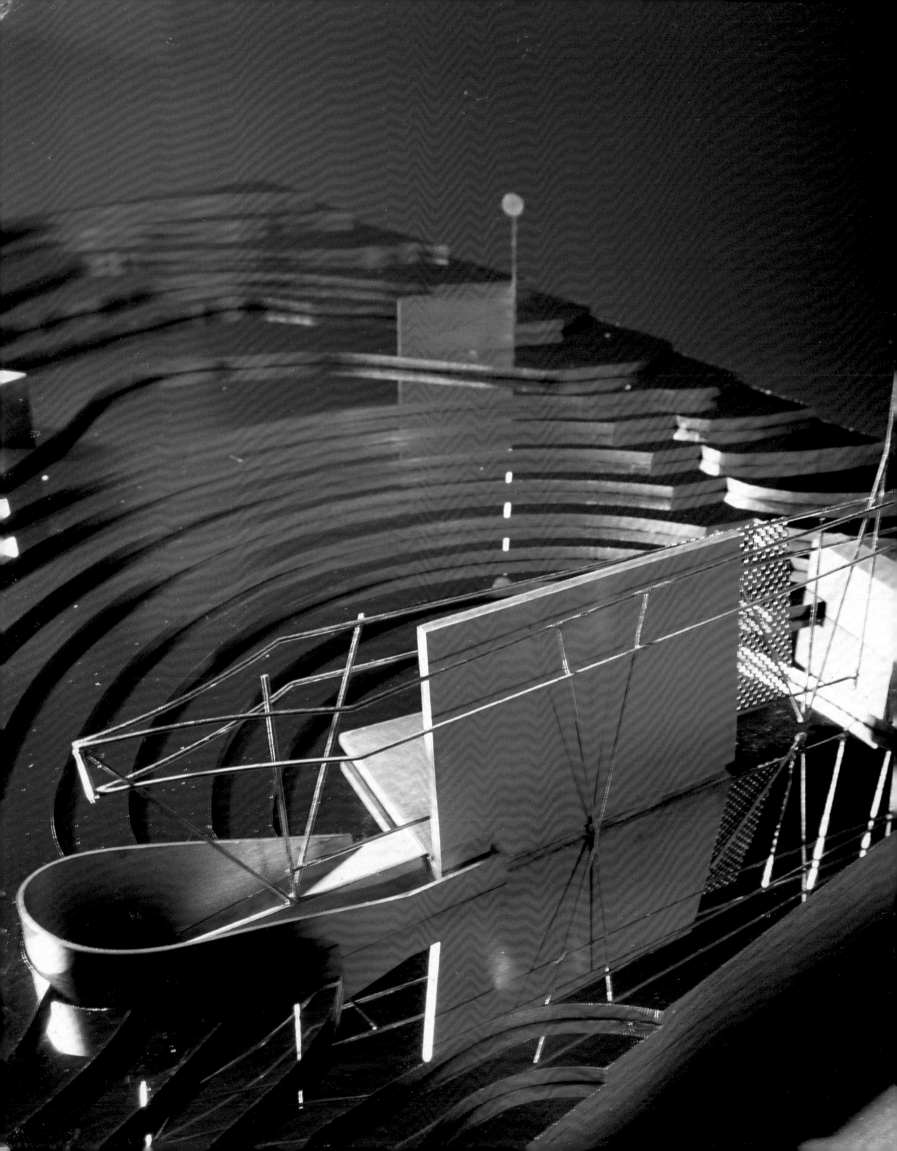

PFAFFENBURG
Bad Deutsches Altenburg

The town of Bad Deutsches Altenberg is 40 kilometres east of Vienna, on the Danube, and was the site of the Roman city and fortress of Carnuntum. The scheme consists of four elements: the extension to the existing museum; the museum pavilion; an open air theatre and a belvedere.

These are linked by a series of ley lines, with the existing church tower and Turkish burial mound, to form a six point lattice that can be lit at night by lasers. The geometry of the lattice also generates certain parts of the building detail.

The Insertions – A Series of Small Structures

The key to these structures lies in the mysteries and memories: found sometimes on the ground and sometimes within the ground: The Roman relics, the incidental configuration of small buildings, paths, enclosures and mysterious marks exist amongst the hillside above Bad Deutsches Altenburg.

Each insertion will establish itself as a rectilinear steel mask: the main museum extension a vertical mask; the museum pavilion a slightly inclined mask; the theatre backdrop a more inclined mask and the base of the belvedere a near horizontal mask.

The Museum Extension

The Villa Zottman is replaced by a rectilinear mask that contains the key references to the understanding of the Relics. Entering the mask building one collects information – printed, projected, simulated and refined – from the accumulated research of the relic sites.

Walking through to the garden behind, one is confronted by the relics and reconstructions themselves, which are contained in simple glass boxes inserted into the ground. The walk amongst them is in the nature of a perambulation.

The Museum Pavilion

Paths following the ley lines (from the theatre and from the tumulus) interact within the shaft that contains the virtual reality screen. Inserted into the ground is a miniaturized landscape which contains the artefacts of the exhibition. The focus of the exhibition, the site model, will be suspended below the glass at eye level and then visible from above as the observer eventually travels up through the roof into the gardens. The glass roof is envisaged as a continuation of the natural landscape.

Relic Box Display System

Relics are held inside sealed laminated glass boxes by tensioned cables. The environment of the box is controlled by a concealed air circulatory system. Interactive monitors linked to the virtual reality screen in the Museum Extension provide information from the relic garden.

The Open Air Theatre

The earth is minimally cut and rearranged to form a semicircular amphitheatre within the natural dish of the land. The stage is backed by an inclined steel mask. Around this winds an armature upon which are hung screens and meshes: different events can thus be marked or celebrated. The changing room is located below the stage.

The Belvedere

A quotation of the mask emblem, abstracted and extended into the vertical dimension. It provides a reminder of all that has gone before and yet allows both young and old to sit and contemplate the panorama and all that lies in the future.

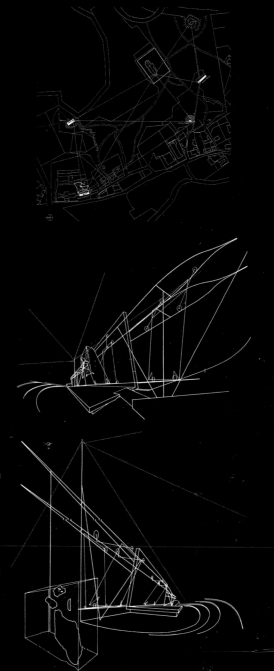

FROM ABOVE: Location plan; perspective – illustrating stage set-up for solo singing; perspective – looking towards stage with relic box in foreground

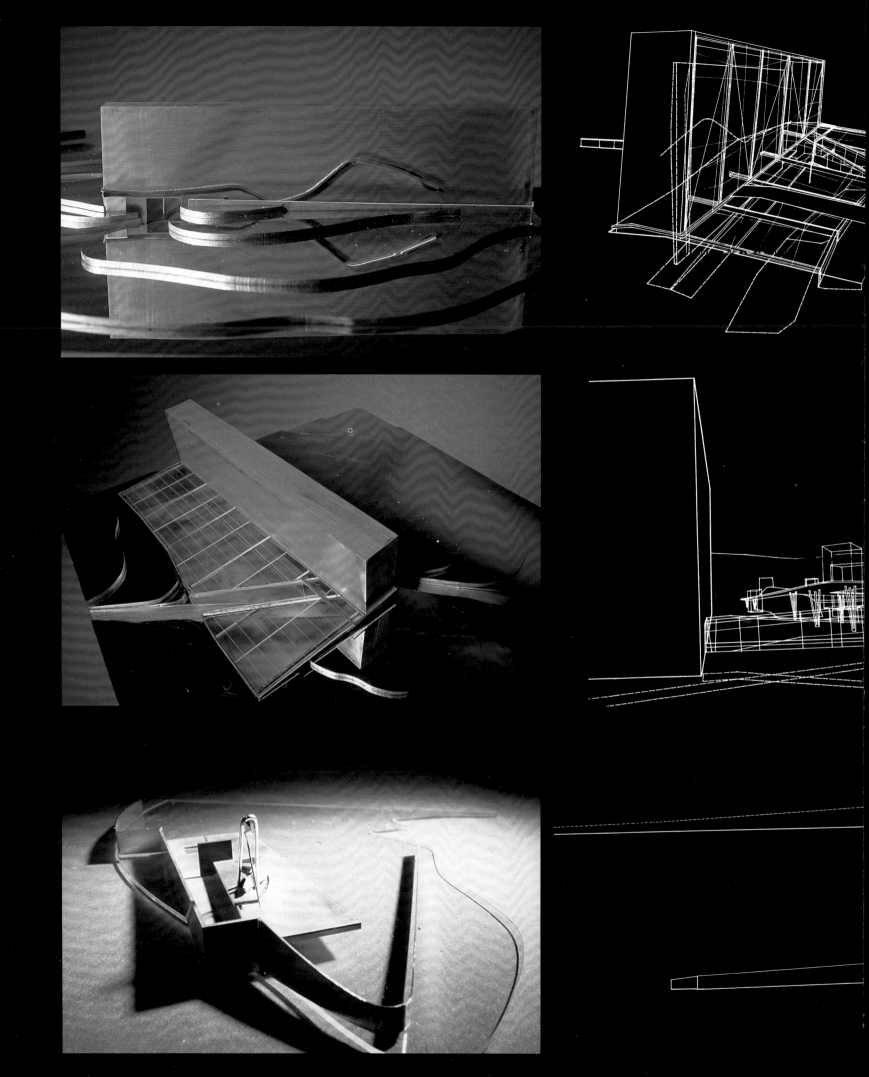

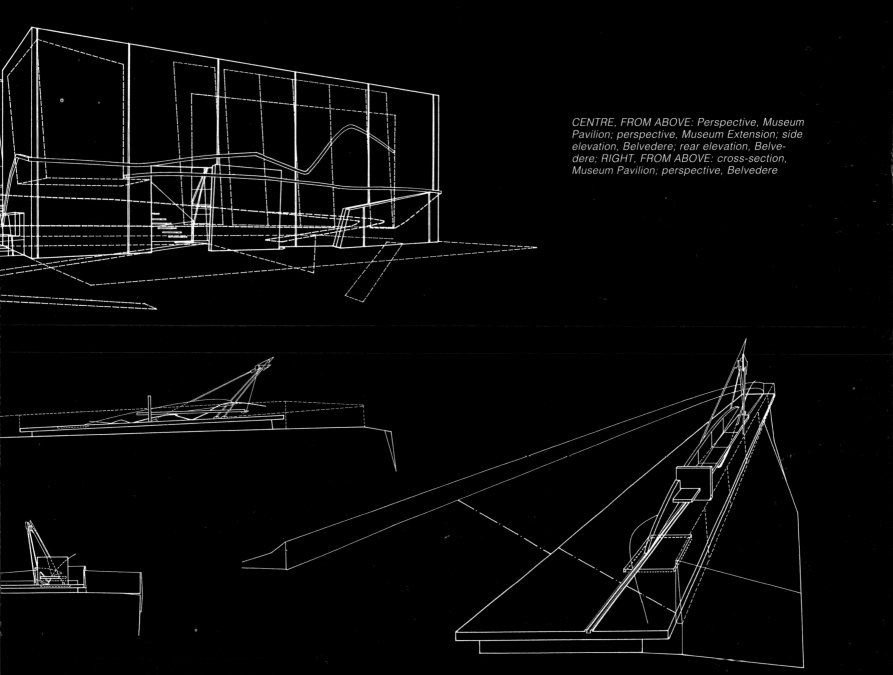

CENTRE, FROM ABOVE: Perspective, Museum Pavilion; perspective, Museum Extension; side elevation, Belvedere; rear elevation, Belvedere; RIGHT, FROM ABOVE: cross-section, Museum Pavilion; perspective, Belvedere

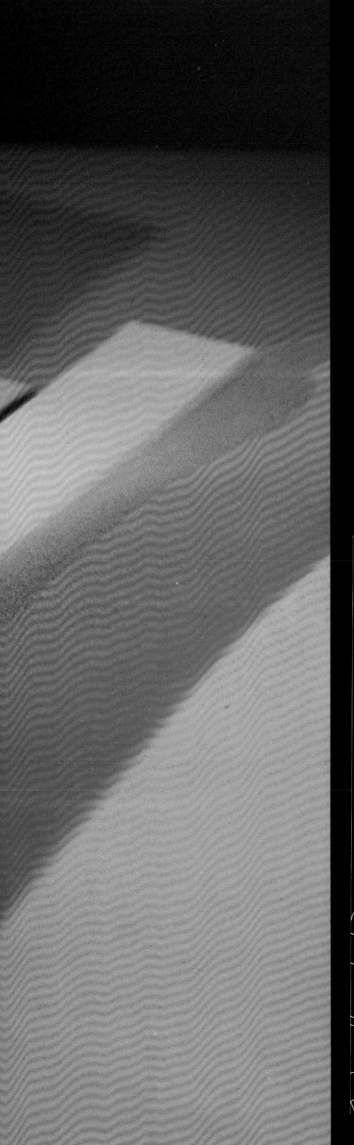

OFFICE DEVELOPMENT
Hamburg

The client requirement was for offices that could be converted into apartments and a restaurant on the ground floor. The north side faces the cliffs to the River Elbe and so the building sets up its own 'cliff': a concrete structure from which the floors are hung. Whilst the south side, which has some long views of the river, is a curtain wall. Certain special 'bodies' are also hung onto this system.

A tall 'gothic' space adjoins the existing building to the west which itself has a Brothers Grimm feel to it.

The project won second prize in the competition.

Site plan

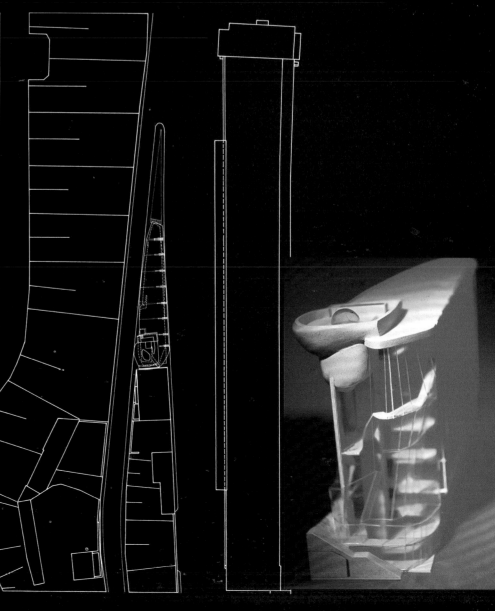

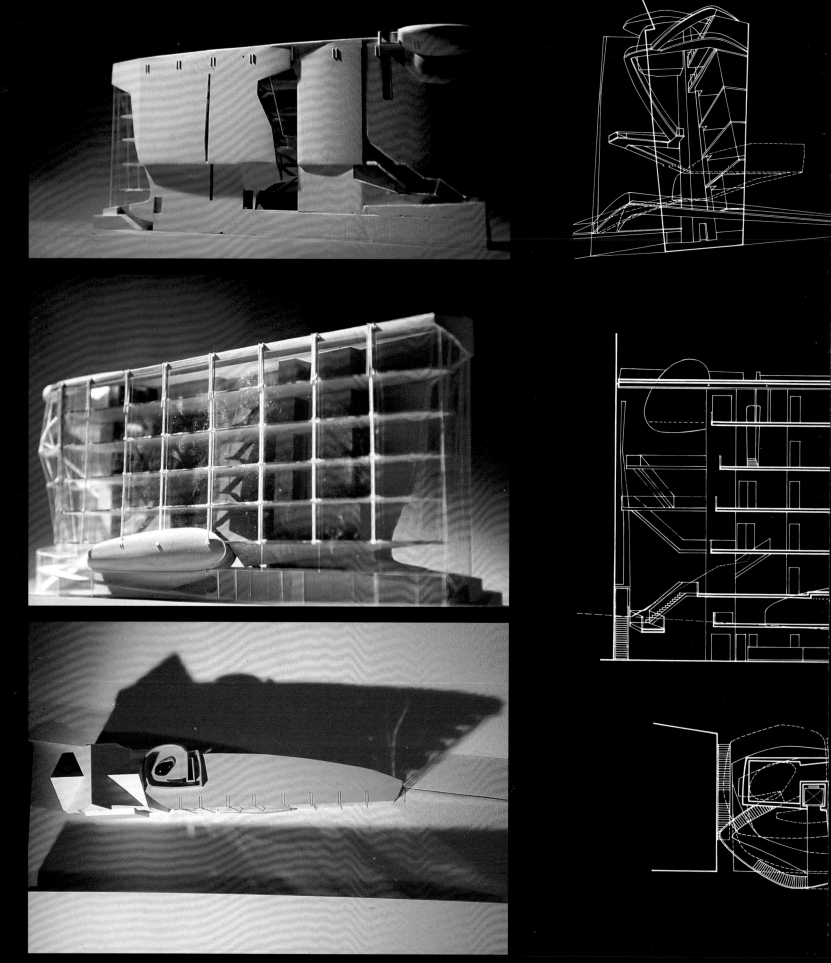

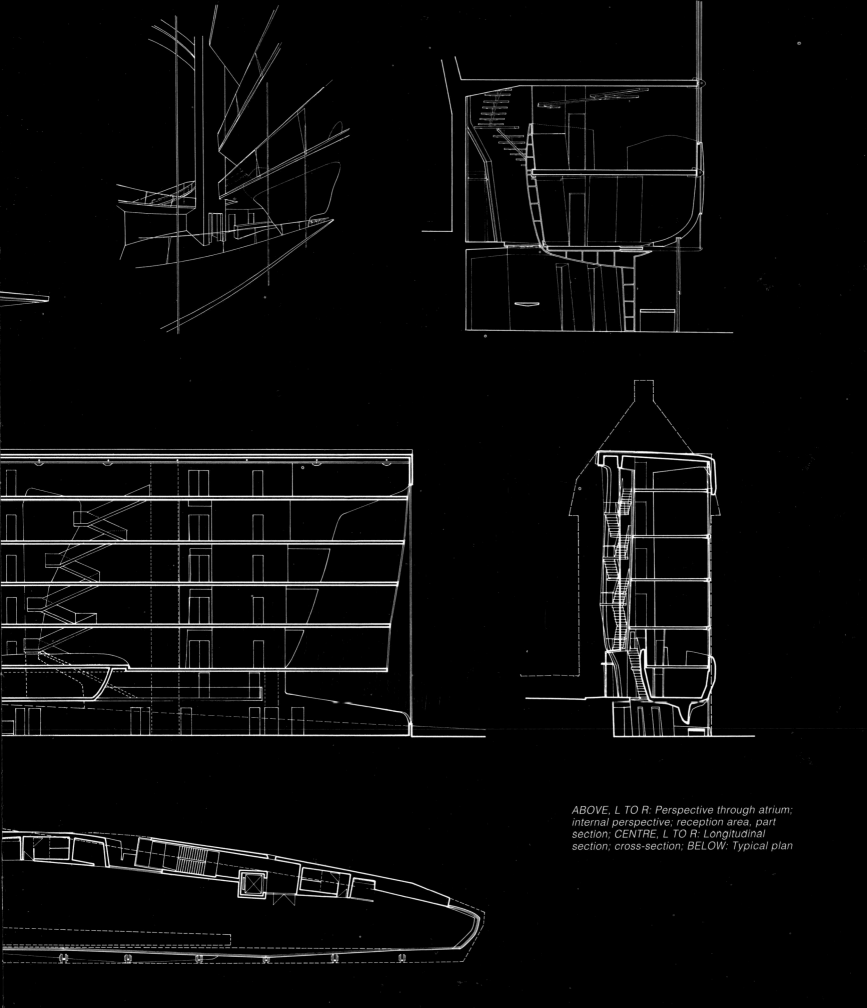

ABOVE, L TO R: Perspective through atrium; internal perspective; reception area, part section; CENTRE, L TO R: Longitudinal section; cross-section; BELOW: Typical plan

MOSCOWHAWCO HOUSE
Moscow

About 30 internationally known architects have been invited to design houses for the Moscow Interbau, organised with the International Academy of Architecture (of which Peter Cook is an Academician). In parallel, there has been an open competition for Russian architects to design houses for the Interbau.

A park area to the west of Moscow has been donated for the whole development of some 50 or more houses, and the brief is for a 'villa' with swimming-pool and sufficient room for a family and two cars.

The design is based on the notions of climate and living as experience. Out of this comes the development of fundamental principles regarding the catching of the sun and digging in against the cold. In their 'Blue House' of 1980, Cook and Hawley created a system of *trombe* walls, heat up chambers and a very solid north side. In the Moscowhawco house, the north is dug into a grass embankment and there is then a warm up chamber with *trombe* walls.

The living space is based around the possibilities of audio-visual techniques incorporating views of the garden. The basic plan is circular: a rotatable disc that can face the family furniture towards the east (the 'Spring Garden'), the south (the 'Summer Pool'), the west (the Autumn Garden') or the north (inwards to the media wall with 'cinema sound' et cetera). A series of screens, dampers, and windows act like layered bedclothes to this major space, whilst the library is a secluded enclave with its own relationship to the gardens.

The Cook and Hawley preoccupation with 'glimpsed views' from one space to another (used first in the Berlin Lutzowplatz housing) is developed further, so that the family can be aware of each other without interference. Restricted views outwards are also compatible with the need to conserve heat in the deep winter of Moscow and keep cool in the extremely hot midsummer. Hence the window configuration to the north.

OPPOSITE, FROM ABOVE: Section; exterior perspective; section through living space; BELOW: Ground floor plan

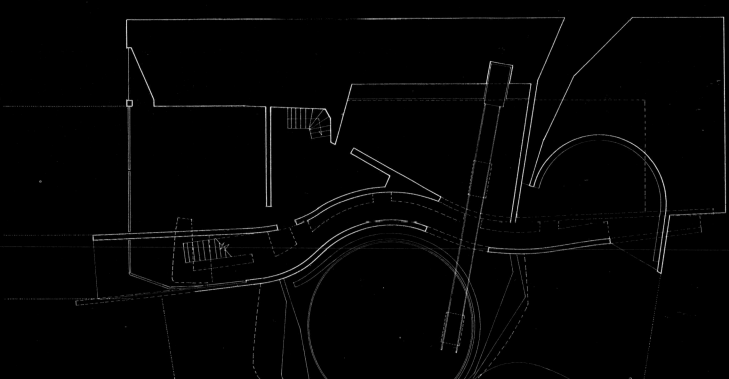

WILLIAM ALSOP
EXILE PAR EXCELLENCE

I started my practice at 9.30 am on Monday 20 August 1979 – two months later Mrs Thatcher and the Conservative Party won the general election and have been in power ever since. This was the start of an exile from my own country.

It is true that I have executed some commissions in the UK, but it is to Europe in the main that I have been forced to seek work. Generally, the architect continues to enjoy a certain respect for what he does, combined with an openness towards the form that the work might take. As the grip of monetarism and market forces have taken hold of decision making in the British Isles, the role of the manager has increased in importance. Personally, I find this an absolute insult to myself and my profession.

It is hard to believe that the philistine has been elevated to a position of power that all too often determines the way we live. The idea of quality, responsibility to environment and care are secondary concerns within the society that has been created within the UK. We are surrounded by poorly educated politicians who do not understand the subtleties and nuances of culture. Indeed the world culture is often seen as a threat. Lubetkin resigned from architecture and sometimes I wonder if anything has changed.

Internationalism has allowed me in part to continue to practise my passion, but I grow a little tired of aeroplanes – in fact I am writing this on a BA flight No. 988 to Berlin. I love London and want to contribute to my city, but I fail to understand why it is so easy for supermarket chains to build trash and so hard for good architects to build anything at all.

My exile is one of necessity and also one of sadness. The real producers of my country are the people with ideas, inspiration and wit. Under CONSERVATISM the ideal is for conformism, obedience and political correctness, combined with a neat early death after five years of retirement in case you become a burden on the Welfare State. MONEY IS NOTHING.

William Alsop

Architecture is one way of exploring the world through work. It must however always be an exploration, not a confirmation. Ever since the débâcle over the Riverside Studios, in 1982, Will Alsop has been exploring abroad. Long explorations have been taken in Australia on at least five occasions since 1983, and Will is even registered in the State of Victoria. At Arthur Boyd's request, in 1993, he prepared a 'master-concept' for an arts-based resource centre for the painter's estate at Bundanon following his gift of it to the Australian nation. This remains a dream not a confirmation.

Since 1987, Alsop has benefited from a ready following in Germany. The Shipfish Office Bridge over the Elbe and projects for a workshop and apartment complex, both in Hamburg, were followed by the Hamburg Ferry Terminal building (1988). The winning scheme for the Hôtel du Départment, des Bouches-du-Rhône, Marseilles, was the climax in 1990 of a protracted series of involvements in French projects (completed 1994). World Trade Centre projects in Nuremberg, and La Maison Europa, Geneva, indicate a ready acceptance of Alsop ideas in Central Europe, but, as yet, there has been no major project given the go-ahead at home.

Alsop has become used to the pattern, and remains relaxed, confident that in the late 90s things will change. The office remains intact and highly motivated, with new projects in Berlin and a bureau in Moscow. There has been, meanwhile, no compromising of standards to secure British commissions. If anything, the work has become more explorative than before, and Alsop has accepted the invitation to fill a chair in Vienna, the most demanding of architectural hotbeds. The practice remains truly international yet firmly centred on London.

Michael Spens

ALSOP & STÖRMER
LA MAISON EUROPA
Geneva

La Maison Europa consists of three blocks and two open-ended landscaped courtyards. These blocks are orientated in order to maximize daylighting into the courtyards whilst minimizing external noise and solar gain.

Overall the gross floor area is approximately 29,000m², excluding underground levels, which include 240 car-park spaces – there are only seven above ground. The structural grid for each block is derived in order to optimize the planning efficiency of the below ground car-park and the cost of the concrete frame above ground. The superstructure of each block is simple and expensive, transfer structures have been avoided.

The office planning grid of 150cm is proposed in order to provide maximum flexibility to meet client requirements and to allow for future changes. By naturally ventilating the perimeter offices the extent of mechanical services is kept to a minimum, and energy recovery is proposed where possible.

Architecturally, the play of light and the transparency and translucency of the claddings, set against carefully designed landscaping, will provide both visitors and occupants with a unique environment.

FROM ABOVE: Environmental analysis of facade; location plan

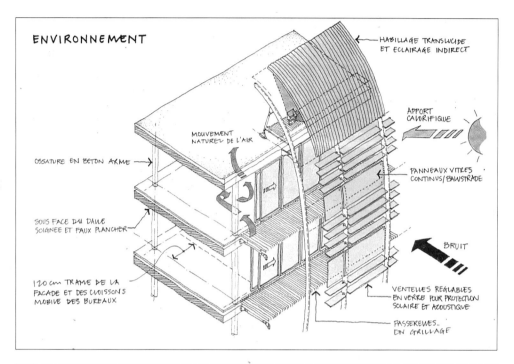

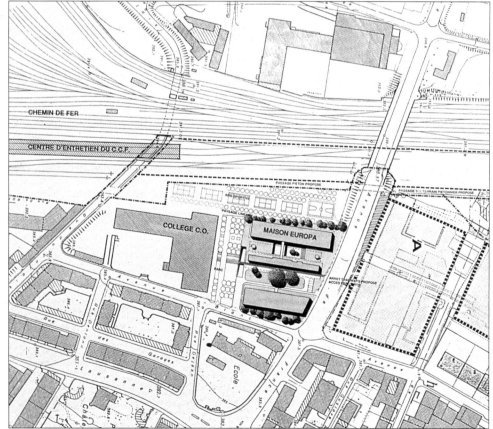

KAUFHAUS DES NORDENS
Hamburg

This project will link, and therefore vitalize, two existing department stores on Hamburg's main shopping street, which are currently divided by a road. A new type of department store for the 21st century shall be created.

One of the buildings will be completely re-clad in various types of glass panel, the other building, however, is listed. A connection between the two buildings will be created by a glass roof. This will cantilever from a new structure on one side of the road separating the buildings, but which avoids touching the listed building. The result is a magnificent new public entrance hall to both parts of the department store. Through the new basement link customers will have the possibility to interchange between the two shopping areas and plans include a new link to the Hamburg Underground system. A new cafe facility is planned, at roof level, which will underline the gateway situation created by the link.

Through these architectural devices the practice has resolved the difficult situation of updating and linking these two stores, despite the fact that one of them is listed.

South-west elevation; north-west elevation; cross-section

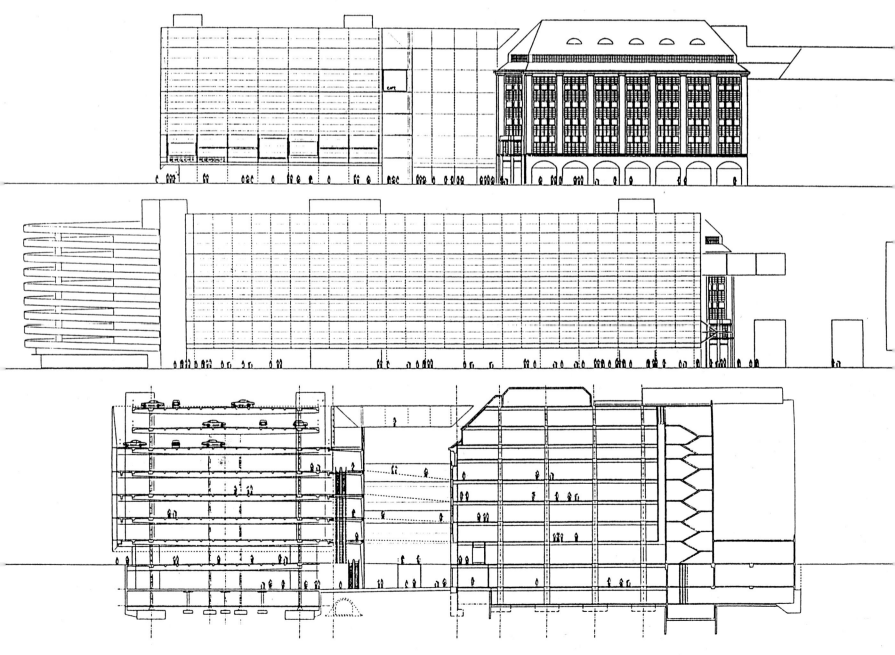

THE EXILE OF RALPH ERSKINE
BOX, BARGE AND ARK

Ralph Erskine grew up in London, yet his roots were already extenuated as his father was Scottish. His Quaker background further instilled a certain idealism, combined at home with Fabian Socialism. Qualifying at the Regent Street Polytechnic as an architect in 1937, he was very soon drawn to Sweden. Working there with his English wife Ruth in early 1939, shortly before with the outbreak of World War II, he found himself out of work. At this juncture he tried to join the Quaker Ambulance Corps whilst still in Sweden, with a view to serving in the war, but was turned down in this venture by the British authorities in Stockholm. Further efforts to assist in the formation of a similar, Swedish based venture also failed.

Erskine's exile was by choice. In architectural terms this inclination is epitomized by the small, single storey house built for his wife Ruth and himself in the winter of 1941. Constructed by spring 1942, and employing local stone together with bricks from an old kiln nearby, 'The Box' as it was dubbed was a firm and unequivocal statement of commitment by the Erskines to a new life in their adopted country. This house at Lissma contained many fundamental ideas and principles, crammed into its small volume, which was formed into two spaces. The living space was also used as a bedroom and studio space. The bed, also utilizable as a sofa, could be raised and lowered, allowing an open floor space when required. The work desk could be folded up within the storage wall, which occupied the whole length of the north side, and assisted the neatly stacked end-on logs in providing a natural insulation barrier to the extreme cold outside. The kitchen was off the living space, but there was no bathroom or running water. All water supplies were drawn from the nearby well.

The Box, stood deep in a forest on a remote hillside, and the Erskines reached the local shop on skis, carrying supplies on their backs, or whenever required, on a horse drawn sledge. Erskine had thus developed a *modus vivendi* that integrated the simplicities of rural life with the minimal provisions of the mind of the true exile. The hearth there became a paradigm for basic shelter, but the practices of exile already persisted in an array of attitudes about a 'better life'. Unlike the shared image of millions of post-80s Europeans and Americans, this was not a materialist or consumer contrived dream: it was one which considered the basic principles of the human condition. From this outpost, Erskine threw himself into a whole series of competitions (11 in the first year there) and gradually got a foothold in the new country, thus securing the foundations for his future success.

About ten years later, Erskine sought and found a second space, a further symbol (although this was a subconscious yearning) of the condition of exile. Erskine bought the old Thames barge 'Verona' at Deptford, close to London, and with a crew to assist, sailed the vessel across the North Sea to Sweden. After some trials and tribulations ('Verona' being flat bottomed) the new space was moored safely at Drottningholm outside, Stockholm, as an annexe to Erskine's office – one which each summer thence would sail out to another location to house the complement of 'work load' for the summer months.

'Verona' stayed as a symbol of that other aspect of exile, the urge to return, or move on where necessary. The originality of the designs which poured out of the barge's hold confirmed how exiles, like prophets, bring messages and truths that their less adventurous colleagues miss. The boat never left Sweden again, but nevertheless it contained the unused option of Erskine's departure and return to London. A symbol not of rest but of passage, always there on Lake Malaren.

For over 50 years of professional practice Erskine's career has remained founded on a continuous flow of projects in Sweden, Germany, France and Italy. He has, however, returned occasionally, and temporarily, to England. The highly innovative and successful housing scheme at Byker, Newcastle (1969-81) was developed after a much praised housing scheme for Clare College Cambridge (1968-9). Finally in 1989-91, came the 'Ark', a uniquely original office development at Hammersmith, London, as yet unoccupied, standing as a symbol of hope at least for office workers in a sea of urban desolation.

The Box is now restored in Sweden, as a listed building, and the Barge remains comfortably moored, more and more permanently, on Lake Malaren. However, the Ark perhaps represents best that quality of hope, that practice of humanism so fundamental to Erskine's beliefs, pushed out on his last adventure, like a Viking memory on an island site, in the land he left for better things.

Michael Spens

OPPOSITE ABOVE: Ralph Erskine in collaboration with Lennart Bergstrom and Rock Townsend, the Ark, Hammersmith; OPPOSITE BELOW: Ralph Erskine, The Box (Restored), Sweden; ABOVE: Ralph Erskine – photographed inside The Box

SIR NORMAN FOSTER
LYCÉE POLYVALENT
Fréjus

Fréjus is a rapidly expanding town on the Côte d'Azure in southern France, and the need for a *lycée polyvalent* was identified in response to the increasing population in the area. This institution offers a partly vocational education to 900 students, in their final three years of school, providing traditional and specialized classrooms.

Located on a hill, the building is linear in form, two storeys high and exploits the fine views of the sea to the south. Internally the design establishes a 'street' with all the classrooms opening off it, creating a social focus for the *lycée*. Externally, the building is tied into the landscape by the use of planting, with the forms of the trees echoing the sweep of the roof.

Climatic control within the building utilizes techniques inspired by traditional Arabic architecture. A concrete structure provides thermal mass in order to equalize temperature variations, and the lofty internal street creates a solar chimney which enhances natural air flow avoiding the need to mechanically ventilate the building. Traditional features such as brise-soleil are also used to shade the southern elevation.

The need for rapid construction was solved by using a repetitive concrete frame, which permitted construction to follow in logical phases one after another, maximizing efficiency on site. This repetition, not only reduced construction time but also minimized construction costs, and as a result the building was completed within the client's time frame, August 1993, and under budget.

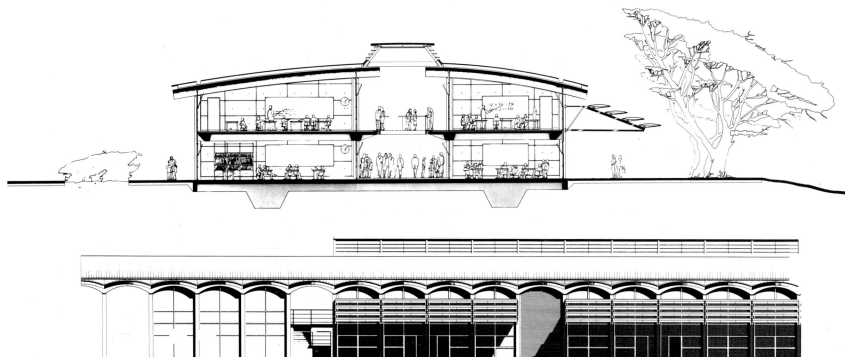

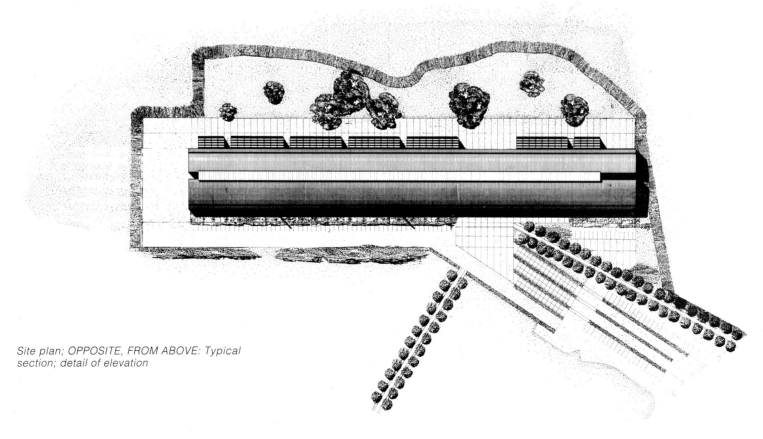

Site plan; OPPOSITE, FROM ABOVE: Typical
section; detail of elevation

MICHAEL WILFORD & ASSOCIATES

UCI SCIENCE LIBRARY

California

The Irvine campus of the University of California is situated amongst the rolling hills and canyons of the former Irvine cattle ranch, three miles inland from Newport Beach and 40 miles south of Los Angeles. The 1963 Pereira master plan established a large circular park as the heart of the campus with six academic quadrangles and an administrative gateway radiating from it into the surrounding landscape. The edge of the park is defined by a ring mall providing pedestrian and cycle connections between the quadrangles. Parking and service yards are accessed from an outer ring road, confining vehicular traffic to the edges of the campus. Each quadrangle is organised around a linear mall and the Biological Sciences mall, where the library is situated, connects the Medical School to the centre of the campus.

The library is a steel framed construction, surfaced with stucco, and delineated with a dark red sandstone base and string-course to express the bipartite organisation of the building section. Through its function and location, the building is a campus landmark, visible from all approaches and the centrepiece of the Biological Science Quadrangle. The form of the building is a response to the functional requirements of the client's brief which required a logical and coherent organisation, appropriate relationships between departments and provision of daylight to all reader and staff spaces. Its form also responds to the campus development plan by providing a sense of urbanity, identity and a variety of

pedestrian experiences. The limited space available determined the narrow entrance facing the ring mall and was a major generator of the plan of the library.

The central courtyard enables the entrance to be located at the heart of the building and brings daylight to the interior. The form centres the architectural composition and allows the building to face equally in two directions, providing a defined entrance from the centre of the campus and a spreading, open facade towards the Medical School. Internally, the articulated plan provides direct functional connections and flexibility of use whilst avoiding a 'warehouse' solution. Unlike a traditional library the building does not contain a single grand reading room. Instead a variety of spaces is distributed throughout the building, offering a choice of location and ambience from centres of high activity to absolute seclusion. Clear glazing offers views into and from the courtyard, whilst the sides of the upper courtyard are surfaced with translucent glass which protects the books from direct sunlight.

The circular courtyard, although enclosed by the library, is a public space, cool and shaded in contrast to the open landscape surrounding the building. Visible activity within the library enlivens this area and makes it a pleasant and safe route during the day and night. The spatial progression established by the Library begins an attractive promenade between the ring mall and the Medical School and reduces the apparent length of the mall – the longest on campus.

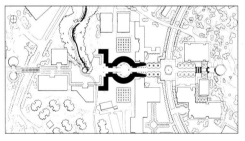

FROM ABOVE: Site plan; UCI 1963 Pereira master plan

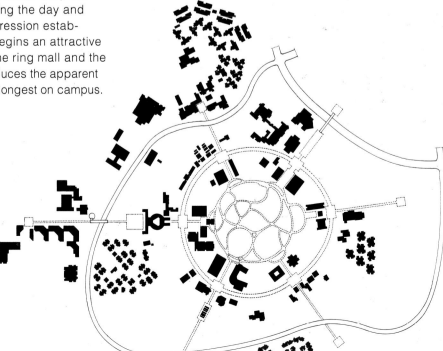

Ground floor plan

First floor plan

Second floor plan

Third floor plan

Fourth floor plan

Fifth floor plan

ABOVE: Computer generated image of the Glasbau Steele Factory – an international competition win, currently being developed for planning permission; BELOW: Computer generated image of Terrasson – Continent de l'imaginaire due to be completed in 1995

IAN RITCHIE
FLUENTLY FRENCH

My prolonged absence from home has been neither imposed or self-imposed. It has been perhaps a combination of both. As an early European architect, first working in Germany in 1970 and receiving my first commission from France in 1976, my interest in seeking a boundary free approach to architectural thought and practice made the emerging European Community a natural setting. The UK was, and still is prevaricating over Europe, while for more than two decades its reality has been central to my life

While my contemporaries were still working within architectural practices, I was off on my own at the age of 28. By the time we received our first large UK commission, to design the Roy Square housing scheme, I had already taken responsibility for several constructed projects abroad running into many millions of pounds.

My ideas and creativity have certainly been more readily accepted abroad, and this has, fortunately, led to our practice receiving more commissions from mainland Europe than from the UK. Abroad, one has an opportunity to approach work with a directness, freshness and openness which can bring lots of pleasure. As cultural strangers there is an inevitable curiosity on both sides and no one anticipates a conventional exchange. Because of this framework, preconceptions, although clearly existing, are given a low priority, and new ways of exploring ideas and the processes required to achieve them come much more easily. Simply being in a milieu of different cultures is an action which brings forward innovation and development. The more we collectively or individually remain marooned within our own culture, the more our ideas will fossilize. For me, my cultural identity has not been lost working abroad, but rather it has become much more focused, clearer and contextual.

I have never chosen to work specifically in any particular country as against another, although both myself and my French wife have always preferred to live in London. I suppose that, having learnt to speak French fluently, language would not have proved to be an obstacle if a French commission had come along. What did surprise me was that they have come along so regularly, while they have been very rare in England. Now, more invitations come from Germany than from either France or England, yet I do not speak German fluently. Participating in different European cultures has been hugely rewarding, not only in the development of ideas, but also in helping one's confidence to mature.

The British have always had a propensity for both innovation, yet exploiting innovation has often seemed amateurish, as if it was immoral. I recall one of our English clients saying 'I'll consider innovation, but not pioneering, pioneers get arrows in their backs!' Most British clients will not even consider innovation. A favourite saying abroad is – 'the British invent, let others exploit.'

Living with modernity, when it is being led by other countries, is given its illustrious past, difficult for the British to accept. Britain's own ability to modernize itself has been tentative, and those who have had the will to invest their energy in the present, for the future, have often been frustrated by a reluctance to back innovation properly – and subsequently emigrated.

To make suggestions that we might learn from studying how things are done elsewhere (with the possible exception of the USA) is so often taken as a sign of disloyalty. For the British to invite a foreign architect (not in including the big commercial practices from America) to come and design a significant building here is almost unheard of. It is only very recently that Edinburgh commissioned Meier, and The Tate selected Herzog & de Meuron.

Why is it, that for so long, the British seem so reluctant to invest in young professional talent? Is it that we are preoccupied with safeguarding the *status quo*, of a misplaced sense of self-preservation? Is the UK's pop and rock music industry so successful because it doesn't rely upon, or invade, the nation's establishment arenas? The reactionary element which is always present in the young always demands or implies the need for change – exactly what British culture seems to have denied, or abdicated, during the last 40 or so years. I have felt that while a marginally quicker rate of change can be tolerated, indeed sometimes even welcomed abroad, we in Britain seem reluctant to accept the premise that another way of doing things could not only be better for all concerned, but would actually be more enjoyable. I am not referring to the imposition of a centralized political dogma, but to a cultural development in professional activity. I find it astonishing that we still maintain separate professional institutions for architects and engineers. Switzerland does not, and I doubt that this is because there are not so many of them to justify separate institutions? It is probably because they recognize the obvious interdependence of the professions.

While we in Britain have been basking in the sunset of our post-Victorian empire, enterprise and invention, other countries have sought to invest in their futures. Has my involvement with some of these European countries, and their government projects, somehow conveyed a sense of disloyalty to Britain? I hope not, but the lack of commissioned work for young architects here has given me the feeling that this country has shown disloyalty to its own.

These are some lines which potential clients in the UK have used in their letters of rejection to us.

'We were extremely impressed with your approach and presentation . . . but unfortunately . . . '

'Your ideas were very innovative, indeed brilliant . . . however for this project . . . '

'We appreciated your unique approach, but we feel that it is too advanced . . . '

ABOVE: Computer generated image of the glass hall for the Messe in Leipzig, currently on site and due to be completed this year; BELOW: Computer generated image of the new design for the winning design for the MERO headquarters in Germany

'We have reluctantly concluded that your design proposals are too modern.'
These are some of the opening lines in letters from various people in Europe.

'We were delighted with your creative proposals and although they appear extremely advanced we are very pleased to inform you that we wish to appoint you to develop them, despite some element of risk to us.'

'We have become aware of your innovative approach to architectural design and development and application of new materials and their assembly, and we would like to . . . '

'I have followed the progress of your architectural work with much interest, and I believe that your work is now of such high quality that I am recommending you to the University of Paris.'

'We are familiar with your exceptional work in France, and we wish to fly to London to discuss the design of a very significant cultural project with you.'

'We are delighted to ask your office to join us on a major project in Germany where your creative and innovative approach and skills will be of significant value to us and our client.'

There is an irony in our sense of exile, as we have been permanently based in London since 1978. Yet, over nearly two decades we have completed only three permanent buildings in Britain – all of them have received awards – and a few temporary structures, including a museum exhibition interior. Meanwhile, during the same period, we have built 16 projects in mainland Europe. In the first few years of practice I thought that the lack of British commissions stemmed from the fact that my independent career was launched in France.

In 1976, at the relatively young age of 28, I received my first commission, the design of a house in France and I went to France to personally build it. The next commission, in 1981, came from England for a house (Eagle Rock) which enabled us to establish our Wapping studio, where we still remain. However, this house was considered avant-garde. Peter Cook described it as architecture that he might expect to come across in California, but not in the conservative Weald of southern Britain. However, this house did receive a lot of press and TV coverage. In England, it is said that you have to be

over 40 to be taken seriously, whilst it is not uncommon at the age of 30 to be married, and to have children. This is considered in Europe as a reasonable sign of maturity, that one is capable of responsible behaviour and presents little problem to potential clients. As an example, I recall at La Villette that both directors of the enormous Science Cité Exhibition Programme were appointed while in their mid-30s.

On the contrary, in England we somehow have difficulty accepting this. After seven or more years of study an architect is still rarely trusted with a commission. Similarly, in many walks of life, friends or acquaintances, who might become future clients, also seem obliged to reach their fourth decade before they have either the trust or independent means to commission architecture

Another possible reason for our apparent exile, which was perhaps more significant, was establishing the design engineering office of Rice Francis Ritchie in Paris in 1981. Although none of us was permanently based in Paris, the impression I sensed in England, apart from our local area in Tower Hamlets, was that we were now mainly involved in France. In fact, the next built commission, in 1986, Roy Square Housing came from within Tower Hamlets during the building boom of the 1980s.

During the same period, between 1981 and 1989 we were involved in major French and Spanish projects, which were undertaken from our Wapping studio. All of these projects, once built, received wide European media coverage. Only at the end of this period did we increase the number of our UK projects to four. In 1989 we received two UK commissions, one for a building at Stockley Park, from Stuart Lipton of Stanhope Properties, and the other for an enclosure for the proposed Ecology Gallery, from Dr Roger Miles at The Natural History Museum. The latter came about as a result of Dr Miles' awareness of our French work in museology and glass structures. We also received our first major public building commission in December 1989, from the Jubilee Line Extension Team.

For us, we felt that these important and visionary clients heralded a change in attitude towards our practice. Yet since 1989 we have only received one further

British commission, in 1995, for the architectural master plan to refurbish the Geological Museum. However, we now have a renewed sense of optimism, as in the last few months we have been invited to take part in several British competitions despite being unsuccessful in five which have been already decided. Equally, we are still being invited to competitions in France and Germany, and receiving commissions from Europe.

We remain hopeful about our chances in Britain. With its lottery windfall, Britain is capable of realising new social projects for the Millennium, yet, so far the signs are not brilliant. In London it appears that it will be a case of polishing the brass ware already on the mantelpiece – the South Bank, the British Museum, South Kensington (including the idea of a Museum for the 21st Century before we've even reached it!), the Albert and Neptune Halls – or resurrecting ideas from the past – including a giant Ferris wheel, and perhaps even a millennium exhibition to celebrate 150 years since the Great Exhibition of 1851, inside a reconstruction of the Crystal Palace. One project which we have nurtured along, a revolutionary spherical planetarium at Greenwich, on the Thames river bank, has received outline planning permission, and now awaits the support of the Millennium Commission. It is unique, scientific, educational and presents a forward looking project for London.

I know that from either my home, or office, in London, it is quicker for me to reach a meeting in Paris or Frankfurt than it is to reach one in Birmingham. Yet, I can never disguise my pleasure to be homeward bound. I have learnt to accept the vagaries of air travel on outward journeys, but if there is a delay coming back, I still get upset. I have been frustrated, sometimes incredulous, at the manner in which things are done here, but I have never once felt like leaving London. The arts, and music coupled with youthful energy, compassion and tolerance, makes London uniquely attractive and a wonderful city in which to live and work – and with its international transport interchanges, a very convenient base for Europe. However, life would be yet more enjoyable if we could have a few more commissions in Britain.

The most striking difference between British and mainland Europe is that, unlike England, there exists, on the other side of the Channel, amongst architects, and those involved in the formulating and administrating of building and planning regulations, clients and even users, a widespread belief that the future can be an improvement on the past. A reasonable operating hypothesis for the production of architecture.

Peter Wilson

JULIA BOLLES AND PETER WILSON

WATERFRONT DEVELOPMENT
Rotterdam

Designed as a catalyst for further development this scheme is located in front of the business district, beside the new bridge connecting the former docks to the city centre on the north of the Maas. What was required here was to bring the scale down from that of the major urban event to that of the individual.

Connecting street and bridge level to the lower quay is a ramp, in blue basalt, a plane that, carpet like, folds over the edge of the quay and into the water itself. Two lower spaces, paved in granite, are framed by this ramp – a Garden of Fixed Numbers and a field of Electronic Rocks (fluorescent red, illuminated from underneath). It is left to the visitor to invent precise codes of use for these elements.

Apart from the above there are three larger scale objects which will also occupy this area. Firstly, there is the Bridge Watchers' House, which is located at the eastern end of the Quay, framing views of the city beyond. This building is occupied by the harbour company, and is used to control shipping traffic and the five lifting bridges on the Maas. Each facade of the triangular plan utilises a different material, red glazed brick to the street, black metal sheet to harbour and white baked enamel panels to the quay. Secondly, there is a steel colonnade and a proposed restaurant which will define the square behind. Finally, there is the Electronic Tower of Numbers, located at the west of the quay, at the start of the Wilhelminer Pier, which is intended as a sign of the coming activity, with the numbers representing the time, wind, tide and profits.

A further planning study for the City of Rotterdam has also been completed which suggests further adjustments of building masses and traffic systems to bring together various developments as a coherent frame to the new River Square. Including the proposed corner building, which will act as hinge connecting the different directions and focusing the bridge crossing, these proposals should play a crucial part in the regeneration of this area.

RIGHT: Elevation, Tower of Electronic Numbers; BELOW: Site Axonometric

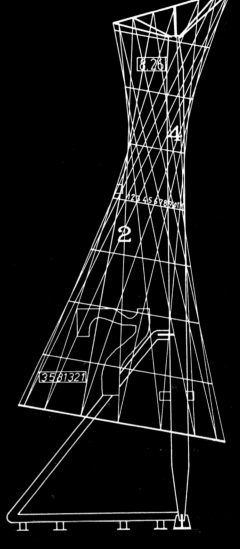

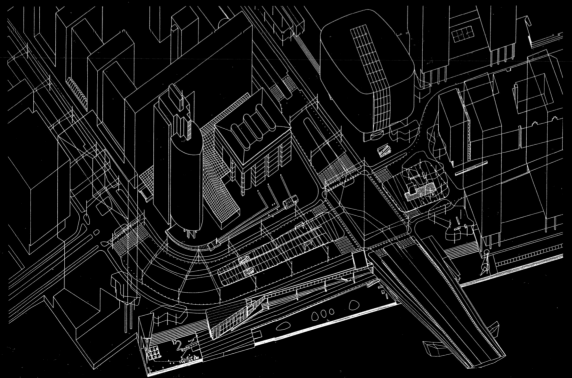

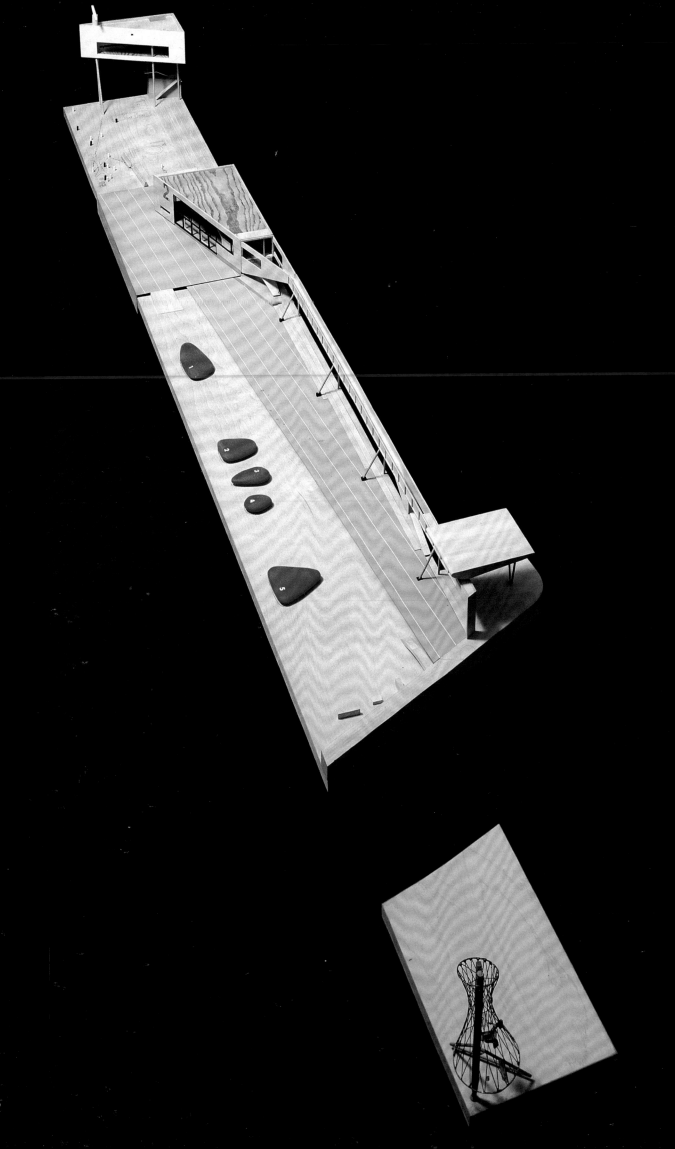

52

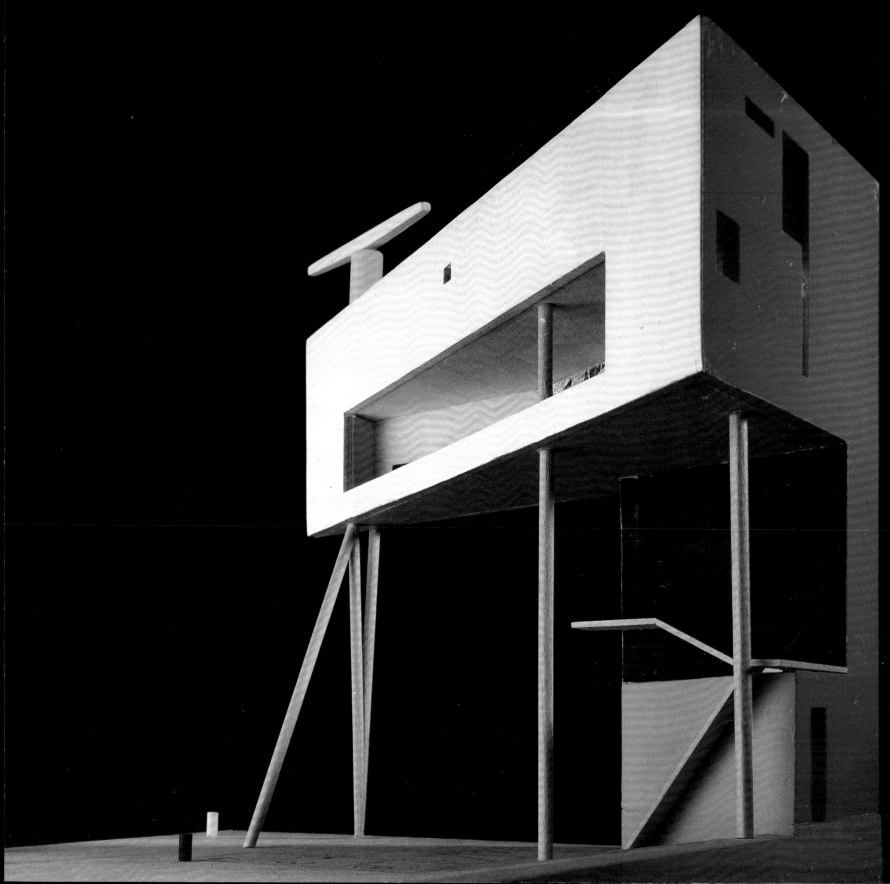

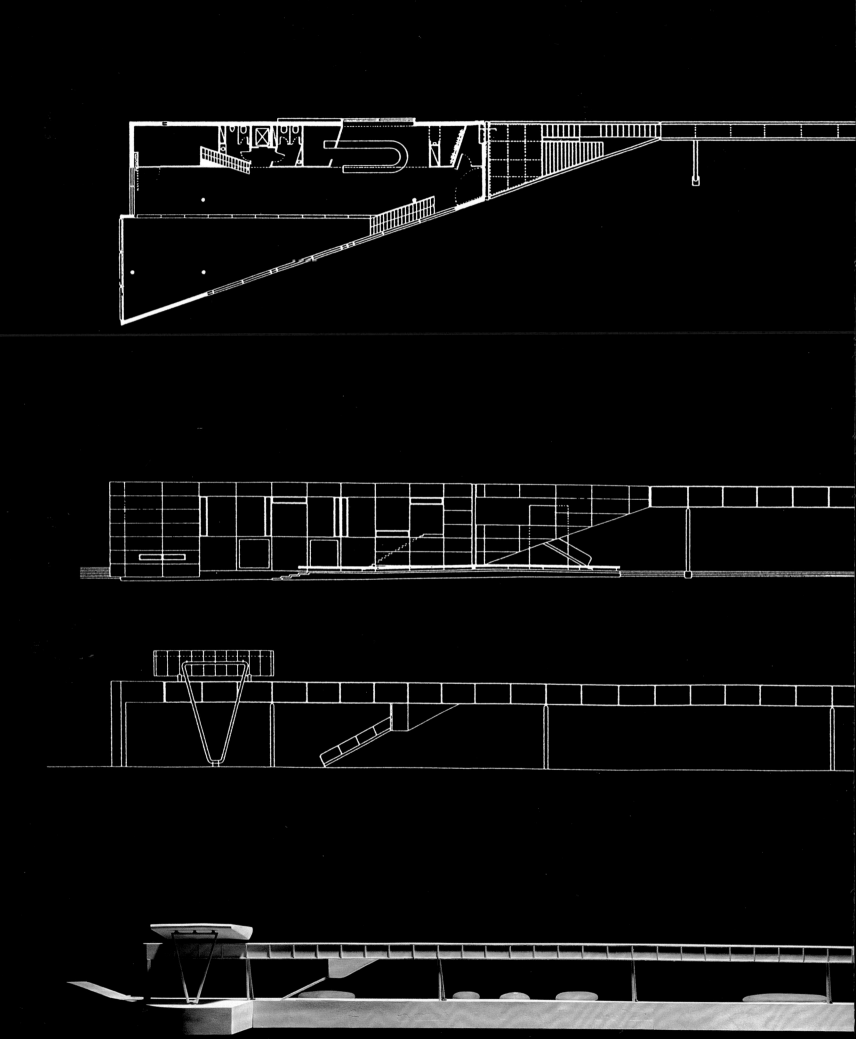

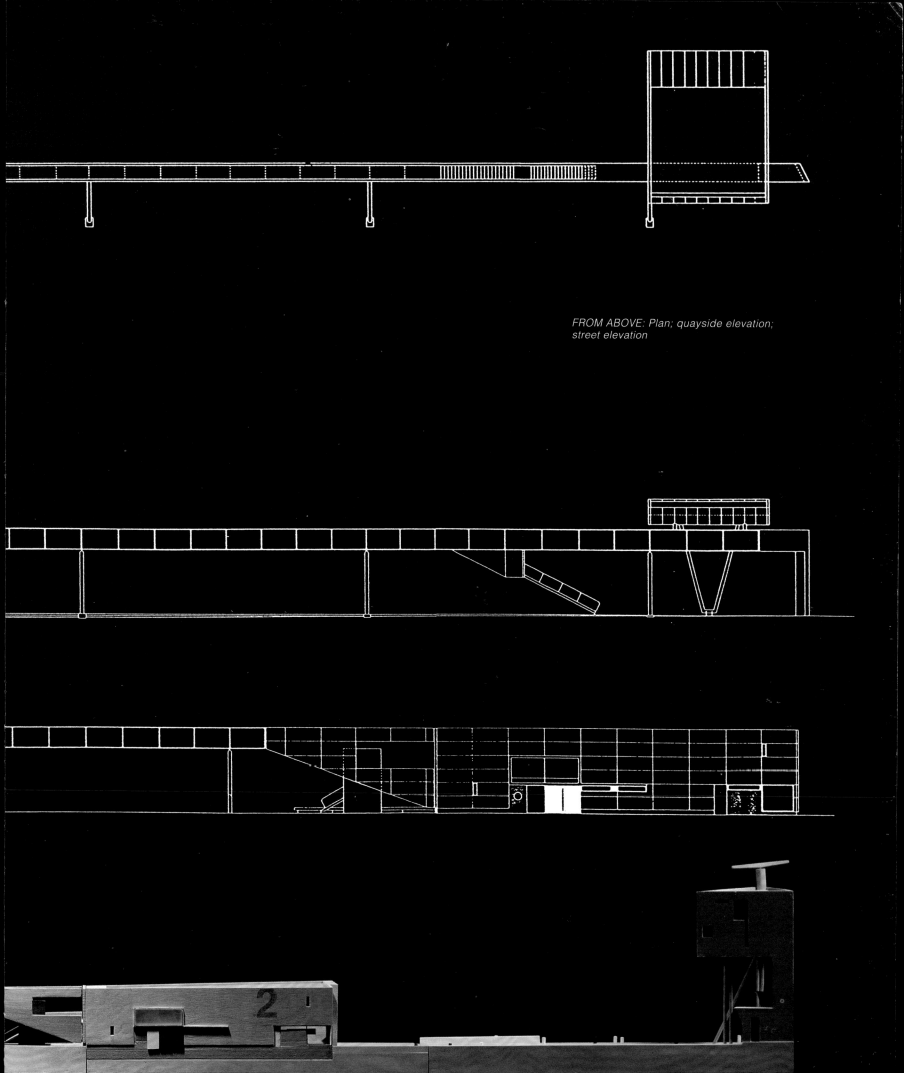

FROM ABOVE: Plan; quayside elevation; street elevation

TOM HENEGHAN
BREATHING FREELY IN JAPAN

Sadly, in comparison to Britain, the 'architectural air' of Japan smells fresh. For many years, it has been almost a truism that a British architect's talent is in inverse proportion to their work load in the UK! Recently all the major works of our greatest architects have often been built overseas. In Japan, the principal works of the three 'masters' – Isozaki, Ando and Ito – are found in their homeland, and in great numbers.

Despite the appearance of Japan's cities – which are certainly not for the 'aesthetically squeamish' – modern architecture is central to the culture of the Japanese. In Kumamoto – a provincial area far from Tokyo – Governor Morohiro Hosokawa, later Prime Minister of Japan, commissioned more than 50 new buildings, designed by Japan's major architects and three foreigners, as a way of revitalising his district and the lives of his people. In Toyama, Governor Nakaoki commissioned 15 experimental buildings, all designed by foreign architects, each occupying an important position in the daily life of the small communities in which they stand. Such visionary initiatives are almost inconceivable in a UK in

which the most popular visions of Britain are those experienced by the Prince of Wales. The ambitions which are transforming Paris, Lille, Frankfurt, Berlin and Barcelona, seem absent in Britain.

Either by birth or by education, the UK has consistently produced many of the most innovative and influential architects and critics of the 20th Century – the Smithsons, Stirling, Archigram, Foster, Rogers, Grimshaw, Koolhaas, Tschumi, Hadid, Banham, Frampton, Jencks, et cetera, et cetera – yet their importance has often been most acknowledged abroad, and Japan, particularly, treats them with reverence.

In Tokyo, a short stroll through the Shibuya district will lead past three buildings by Maki, two by Ando, one by Botta, two by Starck, two by Tange, innumerable small works by emerging young architects and the historic Meiji Shrine: a stimulating situation. Mediocrity, like damp, gets into the bones, affecting mind and body. Tokyo – from its sublime moments to its coarsest vulgarities – is never mediocre, and it is in this context and atmosphere that I feel most able to produce satisfactory work.

Tom Heneghan, Grasslands Agricultural Institute, Kumamoto Prefecture, Japan

TOM HENEGHAN & INGA DAGFINNSDOTTIR

VIEWING PLATFORM

Toyama, Japan

This viewing platform, designed with architects Inaba-Miyoi, is part of the *Machi no Kao*, international building exhibition, and faces Namenkawa bay. This is the world's only breeding ground of *hotaru-ika,* the firefly squid, which glow fluorescent blue. At night, the whole bay can regularly be seen illuminated by millions of points of blue light.

A ramp leads visitors up, out of the garden, to a higher position where they can look out to sea, or inland to view the mountains. The view of the bay is, at first, masked by a long concrete wall which shelters the garden from the harsh sea

winds, and which creates a 'datum' against which people ascending the ramp feel their increase in level. As they rise higher, visitors first glimpse the sea framed by a hole punched through the wall, gradually emerging into the sea wind until, eventually, they reach the security of the viewing platform, which is protected by glass screens. Clear glass shields visitors from the sea wind, whilst the southern and eastern sides are enclosed by opal glass. At night, the opal glass is lit, marking the destination point of the ramp, and illuminating the garden.

BELOW: Inland and seaward elevation

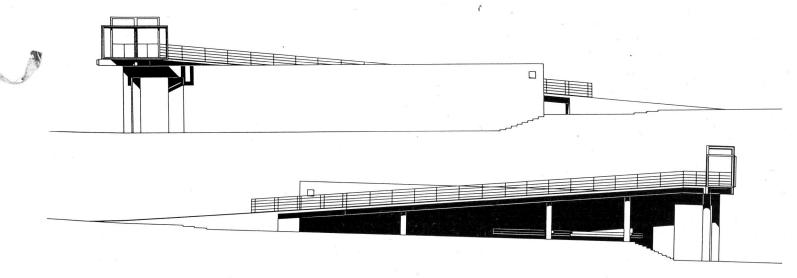

PIERRE D'AVOINE

GONE – BUT ONLY IN MY HEAD

The title 'British Architects in Exile' implies a paradox. I am a British architect practising in London, yet I have, over the last decade, practised in both Britain and abroad – particularly in Japan, but also in Italy and India. During this period the location of my office has not changed, and London remains my base, but I have, to a certain extent felt myself alienated, cut-off and exiled by the cultural climate that exists in this country. Architects in the UK do not seem to connect with the cultural mainstream. The paradox is that some architects are living in exile within their own country. Historically, exile meant an enforced absence from one's country, for someone who committed a crime, which has become the status of architects now in Britain. The value of their contribution to the culture has been diminished and as a result architecture is being marginalized.

The recession has slowed down the rampant commercial development which changed the face of the country for the worse in the 80s. Even architects were heard to comment that no architecture is good architecture. In reality the commercial operators had already set up camp in Eastern Europe and were busy inflicting a capitalist vision on countries scarcely out of the grip of Communist repression.

Britain is part of a western-centric culture that imposes itself on the rest of the world by controlling the global economy. It is a culture of casually assumed superiority which seeks to dominate those people perceived as less materially advanced and therefore less intelligent than themselves. This vision of the world is changing. The global hegemony of the west is breaking down as various other cultures rise up the ladder of economic prosperity – primarily the Asian countries of China, India and the Pacific Rim. In architectural terms these countries still look to western models for guidance and direction, and this has been the position since the Renaissance in Europe. As Coomaraswamy pointed out in 1915:

Let it be clearly realised that the modern world is not the ancient world of slow communications; what is done in India or Japan today has immediate spiritual results in Europe and America. To say that east is east and west is west is simply to hide one's head in the sand. It will be quite impossible to establish any higher social order in the west so long as the east remains infatuated with the, to her, entirely novel and fascinating theory of *laissez-faire*.

He saw the way forward for humanity in the western model of social idealism. Yet in the west, market led capitalism has triumphed over social idealism and Post-Modernism, as a cultural theory, either ignores it by celebrating life style whilst shutting its eyes to the persistence of social problems and decay, or by retreating into an increasingly desperate nihil-ism. In contrast, Japan in all her recently acquired economic pomp is rampantly acquisitive of all that is new. Everything is rapidly consumed and spat out. She draws in a vast and glittering array of performers to her court. For the British the invitation to the dance is a challenge to break out of the confines of a Britain suffering a long period of readjustment, and lack of confidence, following the loss of Empire and the subsequent gradual economic decline. In architecture this is manifested by an increasing dislocation between theory and education on the one hand, and what is actually built and the public's perception of architecture on the other hand.

We live in a world where the amount of information available increases at a rate far beyond our ability to handle the bombardment. Therefore, increasingly, there is a need for re-evaluation and adaptation of our role in society. We must recognize exile as the mental condition of the true architect, and, like the artist or poet, be subversive and distant, yet engaged in a critical relationship with society – sharing an imaginative responsibility for the continued well-being and husbandry of the planet.

Pierre D'Avoine

Small monuments, Maehara Street Festival, Tsudanuma, Tokyo

  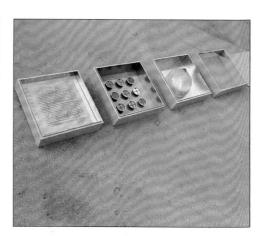

AIRBAR

Tokyo

The existing Café Bongo is located in the Parco 1 department store and is seen as the 'symbolic spot' of the Shibuya area. Its redevelopment is intended to be the 'igniting spark' of the more comprehensive upgrading of all the Parco Buildings to celebrate their twentieth anniversary. As a result of this the café's alteration has been conceived within the context of the whole, and not an isolated exercise in interior design. The wider needs of the store, particularly the entrance requirements, must be addressed by the design.

Currently the corner site, containing not only the café but also the major entrances, gives the overwhelming impression of visual chaos, with numerous elements competing for attention. This bricolage of elements, which, whilst having a 'fun' aspect, runs the risk of becoming mere kitsch, and such an impression would contrast with the image of a sophisticated store selling expensive, high quality merchandise.

The design forms an entrance lobby, occupying the whole ground floor corner, with two rows of doors, either side of a projecting glass box, linked and unified by a circulation area, or 'street'. This 'street' will contain the services and attractions of a transient space: the short stay *cappuccino* bar; the information desk; notice-boards and flower stall. Contrasting with this busy thoroughfare, is a more gracious, relaxed seating area with waitress service. This area has been abstracted as a floating glass box, an AIRBAR, that views the busy throng from a protected vantage point.

Detachment of the calmer seating from the short stay *cappuccino* bar, across the other side of the 'street', as it were, is based on the European model where the seating area is located in the street, amidst the excitement of the thoroughfare. An excellent example of this relationship would be the cafés along the Ramblas, in Barcelona, where the waiters actually cross a busy road holding loaded serving trays aloft, in an engaging piece of 'street theatre'.

The AIRBAR breaks out of the existing facade, projecting into the street and defining the corner. Its form, clear and calm internally, dynamic and thrusting externally, is seen in contrast to the flow of the internal 'street' formed by its solid vector planes. The AIRBAR is an abstracted and universally crystalline object, offering an easily recognisable symbol with a subliminal attraction as a haven, limpid and refreshing in the daytime, and glowing jewel like during the night.

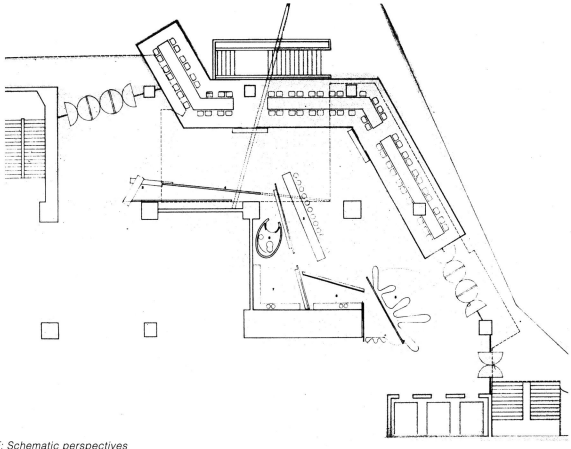

Plan; OVERLEAF: Schematic perspectives

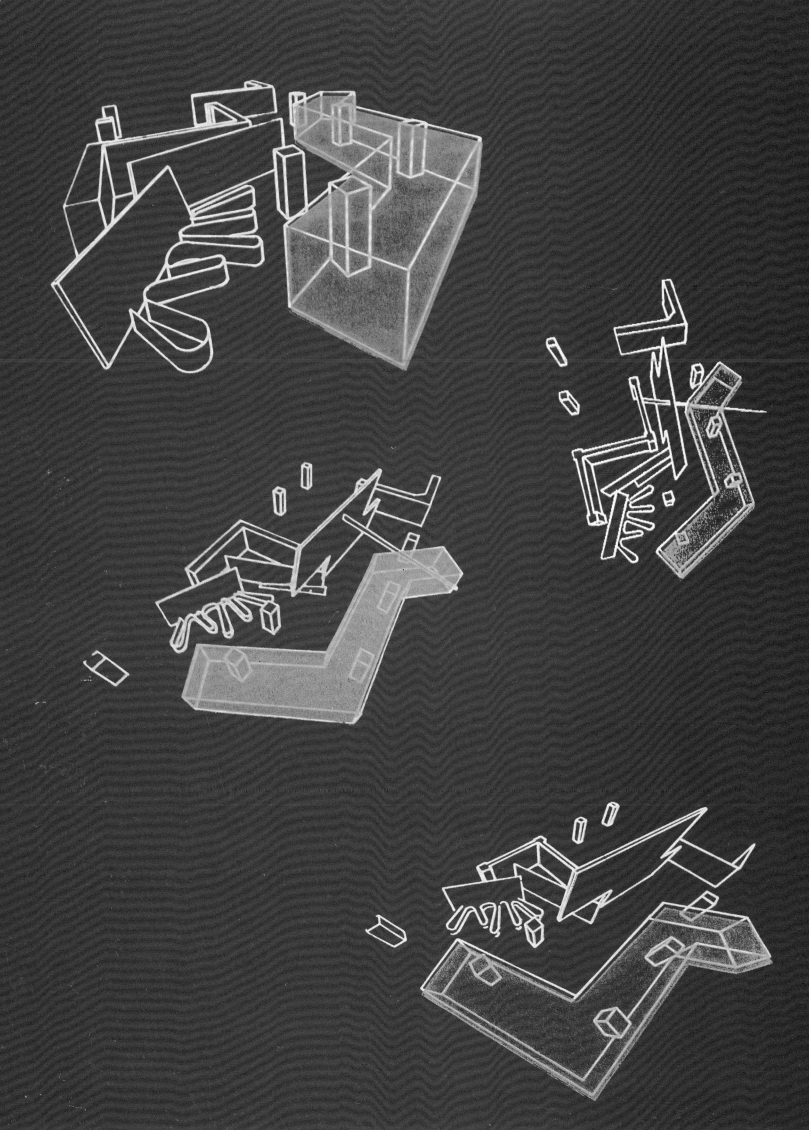

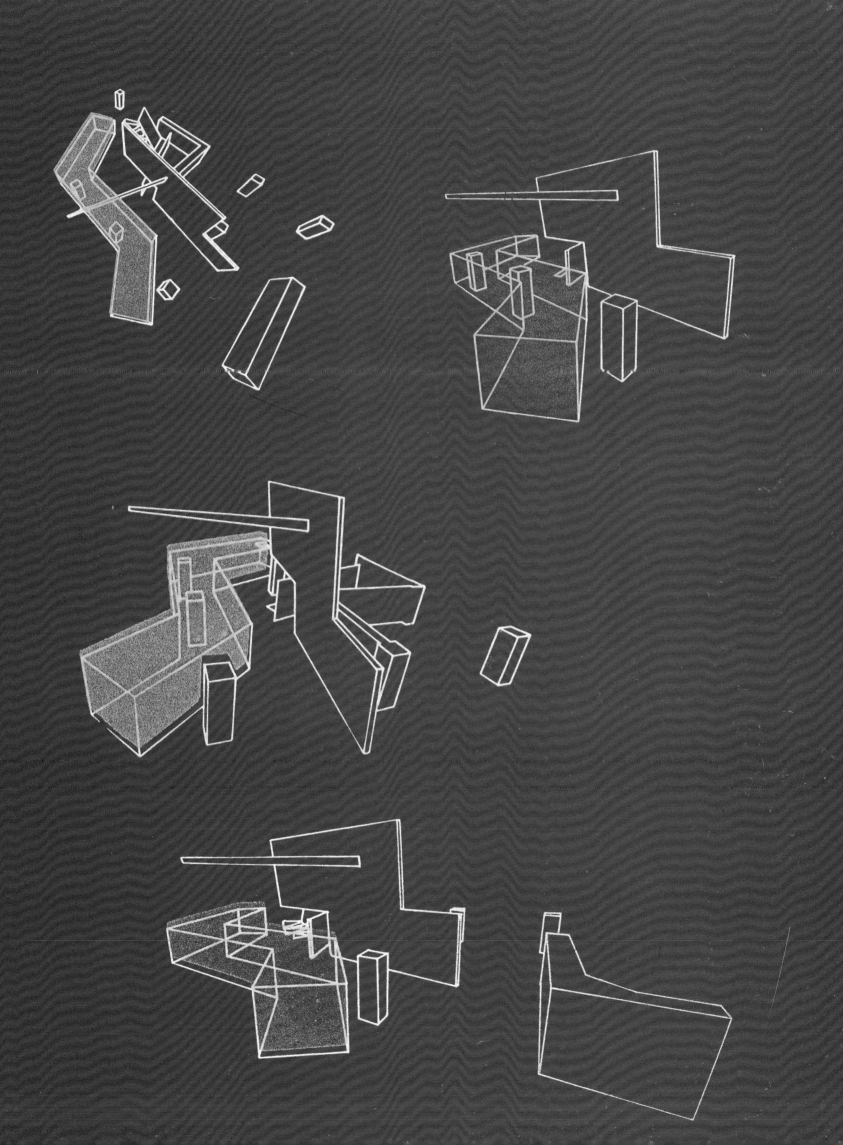

MEHR HOUSE
MAHARASHTRA, INDIA

This scheme is for a small holiday house in the remote foothills of the Western Ghats about 80 miles north of Bombay. The plot is part of a small estate, one of many in the Bombay hinterland, catering for a burgeoning Indian middle class.

As the site provides very little context – at present consisting of a suburban road draped over the landscape – this project was an opportunity to make a clear and direct response to climate and landscape. However, as each plot was being handled by a separate architect, there was great potential for a visual cacophony. The design is therefore executed using the locally accepted materials – reinforced concrete frame, brick infill with painted rendered walls and tiled floors. The house is a simple perforated cubic form, a filter for the prevailing breezes, which is organized as a sequence of interlocking volumes culminating in a roof terrace, or outdoor sleeping space, oriented towards the views of the hills to the north. A secondary arrangement of screens, blinds, canopies and shutters is then added to the composition extending the invitation to occupation.

BELOW, L TO R: Longitudinal section; cross-section; front elevation

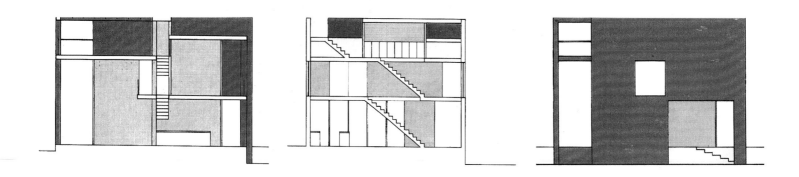

KATHRYN FINDLAY
BI-CULTURAL PRACTICES

How did I end up here? I suppose having Peter Cook as a teacher at the Architectural Association was the single biggest factor in my decision. Peter's visionary and expansive approach to architecture propels his students to seek the great quests in architecture. For me he exploded national and disciplinary boundaries.

I first came to Japan on a scholarship to do postgraduate research at the University of Tokyo, while also working in the office of Arata Isozaki where I met Eisaku Ushida, who had already worked for three years in England. However, I'm not sure if I am an exile. We have two children whom we are raising in Japan, and we are a bi-cultural practice, both Japanese and British simultaneously.

Opportunities I've had here I could never have had in Britain. Mainly because the construction industry here is keen to experiment – as we discovered building the Truss Wall House – because as there litigation against architects is rare; more time can be spent on design.

Our architecture is something which is concerned with cracking the conventional wisdom of both cultures and produces a result which satisfies the basic needs of both. Distinction by nationality is becoming redundant and duality gives us perspective through distance, which is coupled with familiarity. Knowledge from one culture provides a fresh approach to the designs we execute in the other country. There are always stock cultural responses which can block fresh solutions and working with someone from a different culture helps to challenge fixed assumptions and to achieve new solutions. Dialogue is the basis of our design.

Joint partnerships, like ours, are a logical extension of this process and will surely have an effect on the future forms of Japanese architecture. Perhaps the greatest change will be in an improved engagement with the city, and a commitment to a new social agenda. Conversations we have with other foreign architects, living and working in Japan, seem to converge on this issue. Our buildings try to be critiques of their environment.

From Japan, Britain appears to be a place where there is an incredible amount of talent stifled by the past. However, in Japan, the promise of the future obliterates any meaningful ties with its rich cultural history. In the West, society is unruly, but its cities are ordered, while in Japan it is the reverse, chaotic cities, free from aesthetic planning control, are inhabited by a population controlled by a rigid social order.

Many western architects envy the freedom that Japanese architects appear to enjoy. However, the reality is actually pretty mediocre, as most buildings are designed by construction companies, to minimum standards of space and finish. As a result, quality architects ignore a building's context and instead make 'perfectly crafted jewels' which exist in isolation.

USHIDA FINDLAY PARTNERSHIP
SOFT AND HAIRY HOUSE
Tokyo

Tokyo is sprawling northwards, towards the new science city of Tsukuba, with sporadic developments of uninspired plastic prefabricated homes springing up on the flat rice fields of the prefecture, or the *ibaragi*.

The house was commissioned by a young couple for one of those sites, but they desired a solution which might prompt others to consider alternatives to what is currently on offer. In addition they requested their house to be of the 'soft and hairy' variety as a few years before, the young wife, an art lover, had read that Salvador Dali had said the architecture of the future would be in that mode. Having seen some of the practice's other designs they felt that a house of this type was within the realm of possiblity.

The single storey residence is a tube which encircles a courtyard, with rooms placed on this route, like events in a landscaped garden. From the hard surfaced courtyard a staircase leads to a garden on the roof. Apart from plants chosen at the local nursery, the garden supports local grasses and wild flowers, as well as herbs and salad vegetables, creating an edible roof!

When they commissioned the house the couple said that they wanted a significant enclosure for their life together. Considering this it is unsurprising that entering the finished house, according to the couple, is like going outside to a pleasant exterior from the unpleasant interior of the surrounding development: sentiments of reversal that no doubt Dali would have relished.

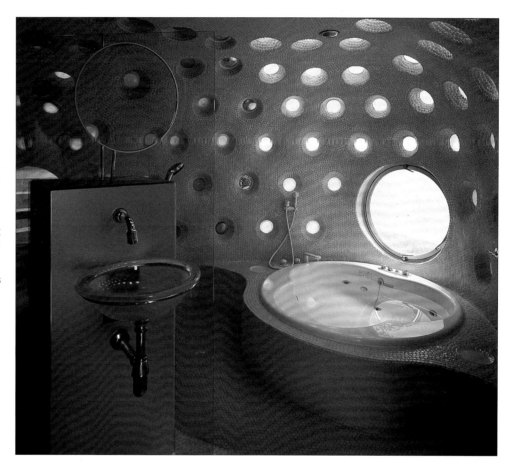

Ground floor plan

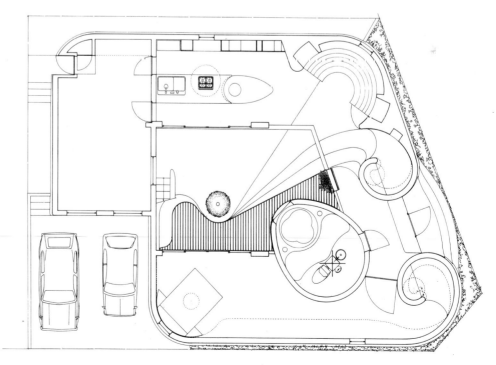

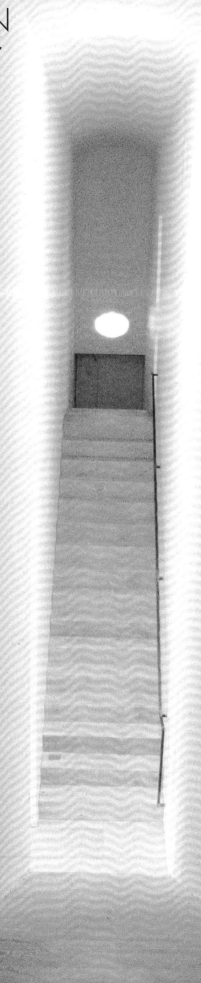

CLAUDIO SILVESTRIN
ARCHITECT OF THE PLANET

Moaning about lack of recognition or acceptance by one's own country is, as far as I am concerned, too boring to hear. I sometimes wonder how an architect with such a narrow horizon – nationalistic, self-preoccupied, attention seeker – can possibly be the poet of light and space, can possibly render the perceptual direction towards the world-scape of a future. Although my office is based in London, my works are located in Austria, France, Germany, Italy, Portugal, Spain, Britain and the USA. Perhaps Asia, Australia and Africa will follow. My international clients and I, see ourselves as citizens – not of a particular nation – but of the planet.

I don't follow the belief in fragmentation: the fragmentation in classes, races, nations or religions. Isn't this the direction our computer age is moving towards? Therefore my work is IN the world and FOR the world.

OPPOSITE ABOVE: Starkmann Offices, Boston; CENTRE AND BELOW LEFT: Yares Gallery, Santa Fe; BELOW RIGHT AND THIS PAGE: Provence House, France

STUDIO GRANDA
AKTION POLIPHILE
Wiesbaden

This residence in Wiesbaden, completed in 1992, gains its name and inspiration from the hero of the 15th-century allegorical novel *Hypnerotomachia Poliphili*. It is composed of a guest-house 'Saturn' and the main dwelling 'Delia'. These two structures are arranged around a south facing courtyard, forming their own private planetary system and in accordance with the underlying metaphor.

Saturn symbolizes the idea that time creates and then destroys its creation, a symbol of life's fallibility. The guest-house reflects this by appearing solid and impenetrable – the roof is sheathed in lead and expressionless rendered red walls open only to the privacy of the garden.

On the other hand, Delia, the chaste goddess of youth, energy and health, epitomizes our modern times with her superficiality and transience. The main dwelling illustrates this through its sun bleached cedar cladding, that in response to its orientation, is cut, swept up, punched out or, as in the east, left fallow. Here the vertical strips, which regulate the facades, are twisted, a feature revealed by the rising sun, that emphasizes Delia's impermanence and in so doing underwrites the tension with Saturn's solidity.

CITY HALL
Reykjavik

Reykjavik City Hall is located in the historic centre of the old town, on the north-west corner of Lake Tjörnin. This unique site provides spectacular views across the lake to the mountains on the far side of the bay, framed by the picturesque buildings on the east and west banks. Considering this, it is appropriate that the concept for the building should derive from the building's location, and respond to its fragile and fragmented nature. By grafting the permanence of the city into the delicate ecology of the lake, an order was established that forms both new public spaces for the city, whilst accommodating all the internal functions of the brief.

This response is articulated through a bipartite composition. To the north the massive City Council building is securely anchored into the existing city fabric, whilst to the south the lighter office building dissolves into the lake. These two elements are separated by a reflecting pond and a textured wall, constructed from black lava, that form an axis almost 60 metres long. Above the wall a shallow channel, fed by a subterranean well, spills water down the wall creating the ideal conditions for moss. This tranquil moss wall is designed to act as a calming influence on the employees.

In the office building light and shadow are strongly articulated and are often as important as the actual building materials themselves. This is exemplified by the south facade where lens shaped columns rise from the lake to support the variegated, vaulted, aluminium roof which sweeps over the building. The play between the columns and the curtain walling of the south facade is further heightened by a tension between the plan and the roof, creating a parallax effect best appreciated by those driving into Reykjavik along the eastern shore.

Inevitably, as light, shadow and reflection play such a significant part in the design, it adopts many different characteristics according to the time of year and climatic conditions. This factor directly affected the choice of materials, and subsequent detailing, to ensure that these changes are controlled and maintained throughout the building's life. Overall, this is a sensitive design that, by taking careful consideration of both its site and its users, forges a link between the man-made and natural environments.

SAUERBRUCH AND HUTTON
WORKING IN BERLIN

Joking with friends we once defined an architect's work in London as 'proposing what people don't want'. Albeit exaggerated, this somewhat reflects the extremely conservative and almost retarded attitude of the public towards architecture as an independent and intelligent discipline. Once there is a client who understands that architecture does not just provide a roof over his head, but also allows him to express his own existence – to 'define his life' – his enthusiasm will no doubt be stifled, and frustrated, by some petty planning officer whose views are as clichéd as they are uneducated.

By contrast, Berlin, after reunification, recognizes the need for architecture. Here it has to provide roofs over many heads, and it is literally shaping the physical reality of a new-born metropolis. Architecture (by default) is one medium which will, or will not, make Berlin a significant place in the next millennium. However, unlike London the public, including the various authorities, is aware and takes an existential interest in the capital's construction.

Given this daunting, but also exhilarating and unique task, the level at which architecture is being discussed in Berlin is comparatively low and restrictive. The ideology of a powerful Senate body, combined with an ever increasing group of compliant 'heavyweight' architects, has dominated the official scene for the last few years. A fact that has been witnessed in the result of virtually all of the recent major competitions. In an unfortunate parallel to London's nostalgia for Victoriana, Berlin seems to be longing for the reconstruction of its past instead of projecting itself forward. The so-called architectural debate seems little more than an endless repetition of the same self-referential arguments that have long been overtaken by the unstoppable dynamics of economic reality.

The main reason we are operating in Berlin is due to our success in a competition four years ago. The situation in Berlin today certainly requires independent thinking architects – although we sometimes wish we could bring some of the sophistication of our London clients to realize the – theoretically – unlimited potential of Berlin.

EXTENSION TO THE GSW HEADQUARTERS
Berlin

This scheme involves the extension, in two phases, of the headquarters of the GSW, built in the late 50s. Although the existing architecture of this complex is somewhat mediocre, it is part of the Friedrichstadt and a clear expression of the desires of the post-war generation.

This building represents an urban ideology which deliberately broke with the historical city, but as this vision of the modern was never even partially fulfilled, the few 'pioneer buildings' have always remained isolated in a fragmented urban fabric. However, since the demolition of the Berlin Wall, the coexistence of opposites has become unavoidable and it is appropriate that the alteration of this complex is one of retrospective integration rather than further alienation.

Towards this end the design attempts to respond to the height of the existing

building, whilst enhancing its appearance through framing, and, at the same time, it helps to anchor the floating original into the fabric of the city.

To a degree, Friedrichstadt has developed an urban model that can be compared to the plan of New York, based on a dialectical relationship between the urban plan and its architecture. The architectural plan has overgrown the existing street grid and, as Manfredo Tafuri pointed out, 'the freedom conceded to the individual architectural fragment is integrated into a context which is in its form not generated by the single fragment.'

This new extension attempts to continue the superimposition of architectural elements from the city's urban history, whilst developing a direct relationship with its immediate urban environment.

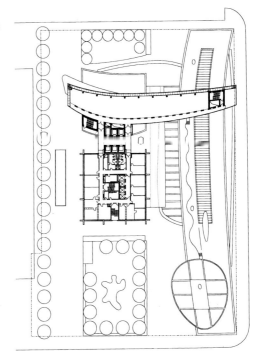

Right: Plan and section; OPPOSITE: Extension to the GSW Headquarters, Berlin

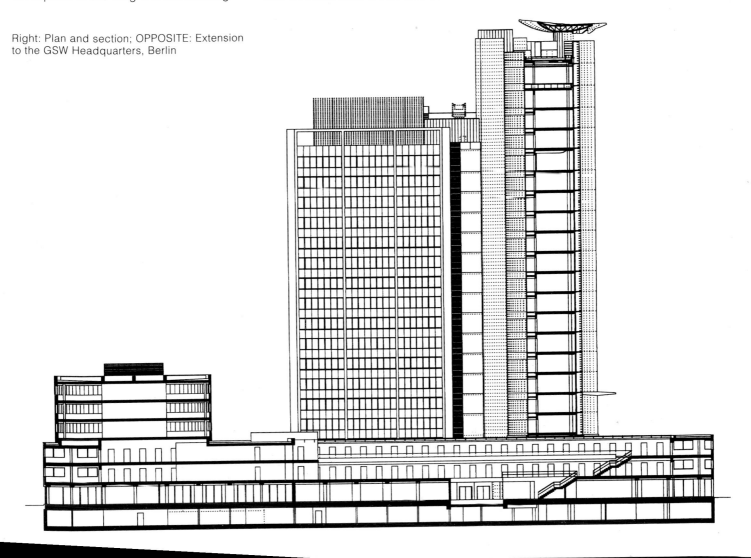

HOHENSCHÖNHAUSEN HOUSING
Berlin

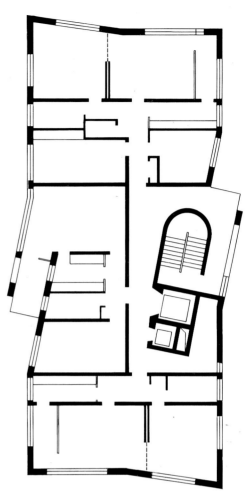

This housing block is located at the edge of Hohenschönhausen, one of the Socialist new towns east of Berlin's centre. A shining example of East Germany's housing and construction policy, this used to be a privileged location before the reunification, so its population is quite different to comparable housing in the West – the inhabitants have relatively high incomes, high levels of education and now rising expectations of the living environment. Ghettoisation of these large areas, which would fulfil all Western prejudice that the degeneration of the city is imminent. Thus there is a pressing need both to improve and to extend the existing housing stock, while maintaining the housing's inherent urbanity. These factors cannot be ignored as they are imperative to the area's survival.

Therefore, rather than undermining the logic of the neighbourhood layout and structure, this development proposes to accept the dominant building type as its starting point – despite their aesthetic and functional brutality. In addition to this it also adapts and reinterprets the territorial logic of the surrounding public spaces and its location at the edge between park and city.

In spite of limitations, enforced by the tight budget of public housing, this proposal attempts to improve on its neighbours without creating any jealousy or tension with the other residents. The result of these financial restraints is that there have had to be certain compromises – a simple prefabricated concrete frame allows for the cost of generous windows and internal doors. The generator of the building's form is an attempt to make best use of the double aspect between the forest, to the south-east, and the open parkland to the north-west.

OPPOSITE LEFT, FROM ABOVE: Perspective; cross-section; OPPOSITE RIGHT: Photomontages; ABOVE: Typical floor plan; BELOW: Site plan

ANDREW YEOMAN AND MATTHEW PRIESTMAN

War Zone Exile

Lying awake listening to the night-time bombardment of a small village on the eastern slopes of the facing hills, debating the usefulness of an architect in a war zone becomes strangely more important than concern for safety or impending danger. The effect of passing a sign announcing 'YOU ARE NOW ENTERING A WAR ZONE' is far more sobering than entering a one-way street at night, especially if it is guarded by heavily armed militia. As a student I was impressed by *Apocalypse Now*, which was visually and emotionally tuned to the senses and provided a commentary on modern warfare. However, since arriving here I have not water-skied down the Norotva, or heard *The End* boomed through the building I was in, as it was not necessary – I was there.

The opportunity to work in Croatia was not an advertised position, it was invented. Following my recent success in a competition in Italy and Slovenia, meetings in Zagreb developed into the idea of research, collaboration, project work and many other scenarios. From that point on Tower 151 set up an office there and, coupled with a consultancy with the city authorities, commenced working on a series of projects in the city. Although informed by our experiences, these are based on the condition that Europe is a re-emerging continent and that America is more 'inward' in terms of its culture.

The situation here is different to London on several levels. Zagreb is a city of just under one million people, the precise figures are uncertain due to huge numbers of refugees. However, unlike London there is no problem with homelessness, as the Croatian government, with the EC and German government, is funding a large relocation programme. Towards this end, our sister company Investinzinjering is building large settlements, instant towns almost, in Osijek and Karlovac. Working closely with the city authorities provides direct input into the future 'planning' of Zagreb. Here, a spirit of

optimism is mixed with the stark realities of an idiosyncratic economy where banks run out and a front line 25 kilometres away.

The last publication which concerned Zagreb was *Form Follows Fiasco* by Peter Blake, a legacy which is difficult to lose, and inevitably terminology like 'strategy' and 'process' have now become part of the city's planning curriculum. As the author of the *City of Devices* programme, the official title for the research here although it paraphrases as *Urban Strategies in Changing Ideologies*, many opportunities have emerged.

Discussion about both politics and architecture permeates both the city hall and the faculties in the university. 'Modernism' is not a style here but a way of life, entirely understandable when one sees the abundance of buildings from the 30s and 50s, which is a fundamental difference to Britain. It is interesting to find people who are truly concerned for the future of their city, but are unfamiliar with the difficulties which are generated by large corporate developments and economic incentives.

The war is obviously an issue, but not how many in Britain see it. Whilst one may shop in Benetton, the massacres continue in Bosnia and the news is concerned with how the UN screwed up or didn't comprehend the situation. When Benetton carried their recent advertisement featuring a dead Croatian's clothes, people were either not impressed or simply confused. Benetton stayed open and the massacres continued.

More recently the reconstruction of Mostar has been proposed, which is both immense in scale and complexity. Nothing can prepare one for such destruction, and the psychological effects of my first visit were enormous. Humanity sometimes restricts our abilities and attributes, and this was my initial response standing on Mostar's central boulevard – now a series of termite structures where once large stone blocks stood. The impotency of architecture is acute, and yet hardens the resolve to maintain a framework with

which such situations can, and must be, dealt with.

In World War II the 'theatre of war' was employed as an axiom for the place of conflict, a phenomenon visible in any one of the many photographic developers in Zagreb – built up by the huge demand from UN soldiers and journalists. Here a disembowelled person is displayed next to a newly married couple, which is particularly bizarre as one can then go and drink *cappuccino* in the main square. It is as if Serlio should draw another image of the city, to join that of the comic and tragic, where Armageddon is featured in neon.

It makes architectural student projects from London appear positively naive, especially the extremely negative gestural work of the past five years. Whilst the British 'scene' is much admired by people here it is simply 'window-shopping' as those that have either settled in London, or travelled there, have been disappointed by the crassness of the city. Britain in these instances remains as it was a few years ago, a perch for economics, export and eccentric connections. How much this has to do with time is difficult to judge, although it has been suggested recently to move GMT eastwards deregulating Britain's control over what is globally universal – time.

Andrew Yeoman

International Style

Landing at Kai Tak and spiralling through the flyovers of Hong Kong Island, three years after qualifying, was an immediate antidote to the frustrations of working in London. Here was a young city, tangibly alive and physically expanding. The sheer dynamism of the environment in Hong Kong was exhilarating: a young architect could be responsible for a 150-metre tall building, worth £40 million and be left alone – there was no time for interference – and six months later the project was being built. To be immersed in such an experience, and to see the direct result of marks or actions, provided enormous faith in the potential of the architect-initiator.

Returning five years later to work on projects in Indonesia, Vietnam and Hong Kong, the place had become more sophisticated due to increasing numbers of foreign companies and consultancies. It had developed even more remarkable characteristics out of its own require-ments – high level air-conditioned pedes-trian networks, public escalator systems, extensive land reclamation and gigantic infrastructure projects – all progressing in the face of imminent political change and the bare minimum of statutory control. Admittedly, the buildings were often crude, or even hideous, yet in their density and brevity, somehow infinitely preferable to the complacent suburban wastelands of the 'civilised' world. Yet, due to its trading ethos and low unem-ployment, Hong Kong cannot support an avant-garde, or the anarchy of invention, and so a return to Europe was essential.

Returning to England I worked for property developers as the project architect for a Canary Wharf office building, assembling pre-manufactured building components in a process akin to financial market procurements. However, ideas to operate from Hong Kong were flawed by its cultural dependency, and with North America tending towards isolation, London, as the capital of Europe, appeared an ideal location to practise from, although not in. Despite the smell of decline, the frustrations, the statutory systems and politics, London does have remarkable resources and all the advantages of an international centre.

In retrospect, this decision seems to have been validated by the fact that, in collaboration with others, I have been successful in a number of international competitions. Yet, here is the crux of the problem. After winning the Ørestaden competition we were awarded a contract to develop our proposals, which, consid-ering the débâcle over Cardiff, seems unlikely to happen in contemporary Britain. Thankfully, it is now possible to operate internationally from London, enjoying other arenas where the output of this country is taken seriously.

Matthew Priestman

MATTHEW PRIESTMAN & TOWER 151

ØRESTADEN URBAN DEVELOPMENT
Copenhagen

Designed in conjunction with John Kramer, Paul Pindelski and Andrew Yeoman, the Ørestaden competition involved the development of a new urban area for the city of Copenhagen, to be constructed over a period of 30 years. The site, approximately 310 hectares, is situated on reclaimed land south of the old city, and the construction of this development will coincide with the building of a bridge crossing the Øresund, connecting Denmark with Sweden.

The proposition for the new township sets up an integration of natural and built environments, phased over and growing in complexity throughout the 30 year period. The natural infrastructure for this will include canals, lakes, parks and existing wetlands, whilst the urban infrastructure will be established firstly by the building of a light railway system, a boulevard running from the north to the south and a series of buildings at the interchange with the Øresund motorway. Following this primary stage, specific areas will be developed for housing, education, employment and university expansion. The strategy of employing open space as a structure for the site results in denser urban areas discouraging suburbanisation. In addition, larger buildings and more densely developed districts are situated so as to be points of articulation within the site.

Exterior perspective

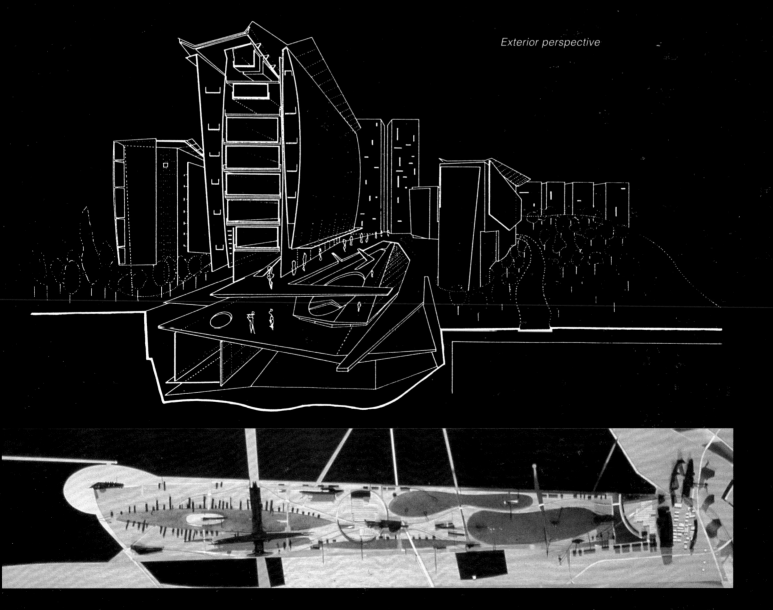

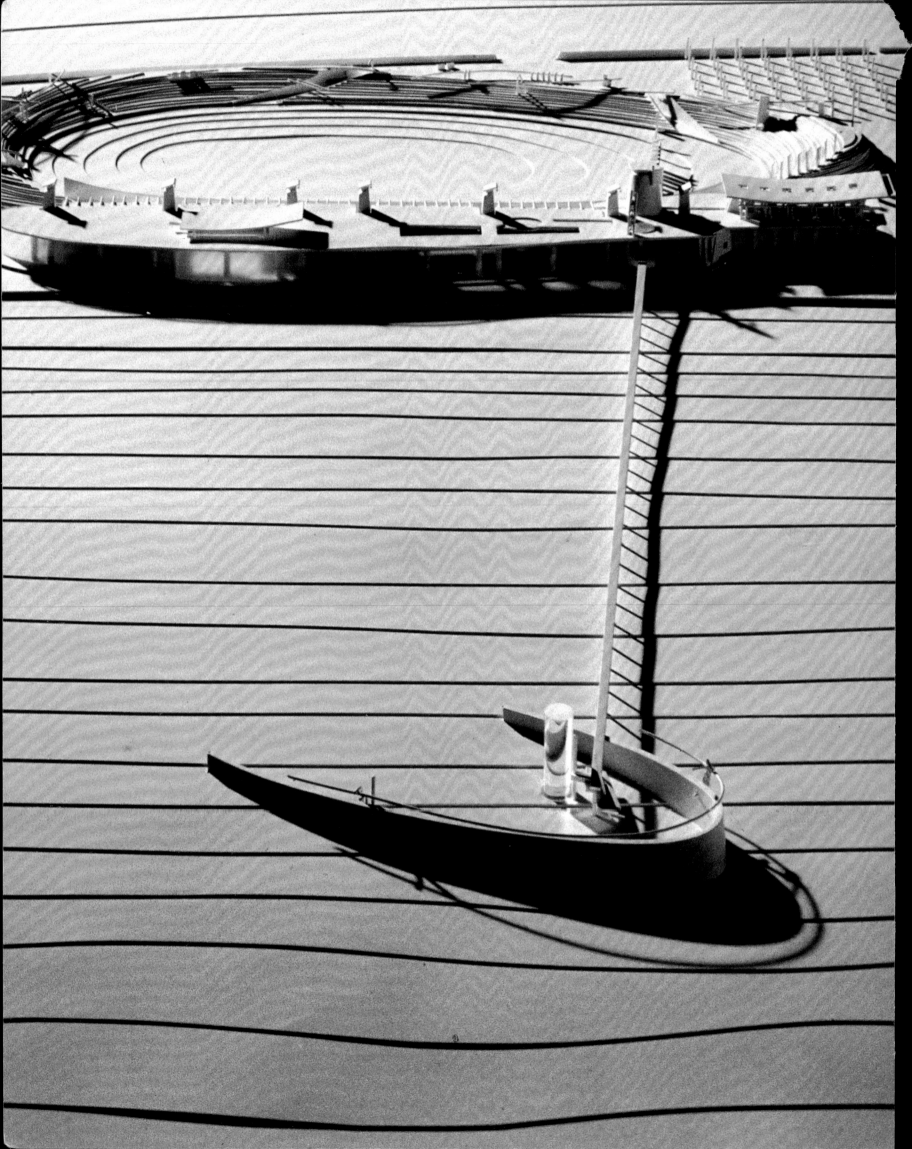

INTERNATIONAL HEALTH CLUB
Kuwait

This scheme, developed with Andrew Yeoman, John Kramer and Battle Mc-Carthy, addresses the issues of erosion and juxtaposition. The proposal achieves this through a series of devices that, when linked, resolve both the environmental and the functional nature of exercise. These four elements – the courts, deck, water and dune colloo tively articulate the placing of the object within this arid landscape. These elements, like those from the Yves Tanguy game *Le Cadavre Exquis*, operate both independently and with each other; their exact relationship being decided by the individual actions of the members. This project evaluates a commodity considered common in the Western world but more valuable than oil in Kuwait – Water.

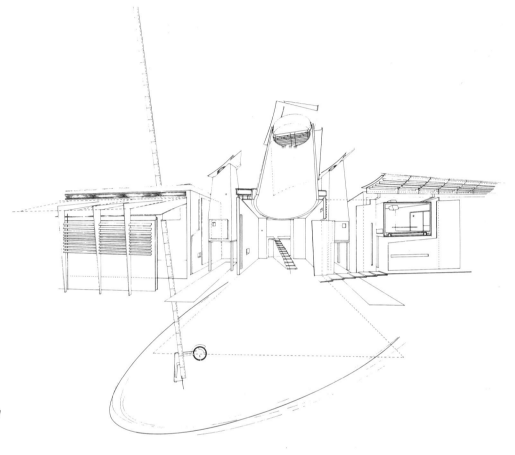

FROM ABOVE: Perspective through entrance hall; perspective of indoor swimming pool and tennis court; longitudinal section

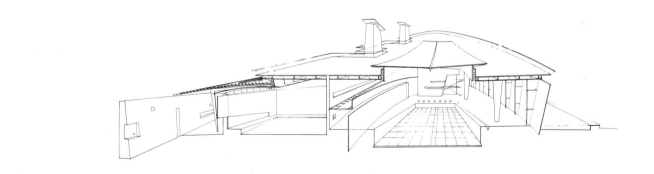

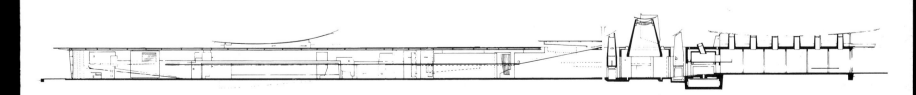

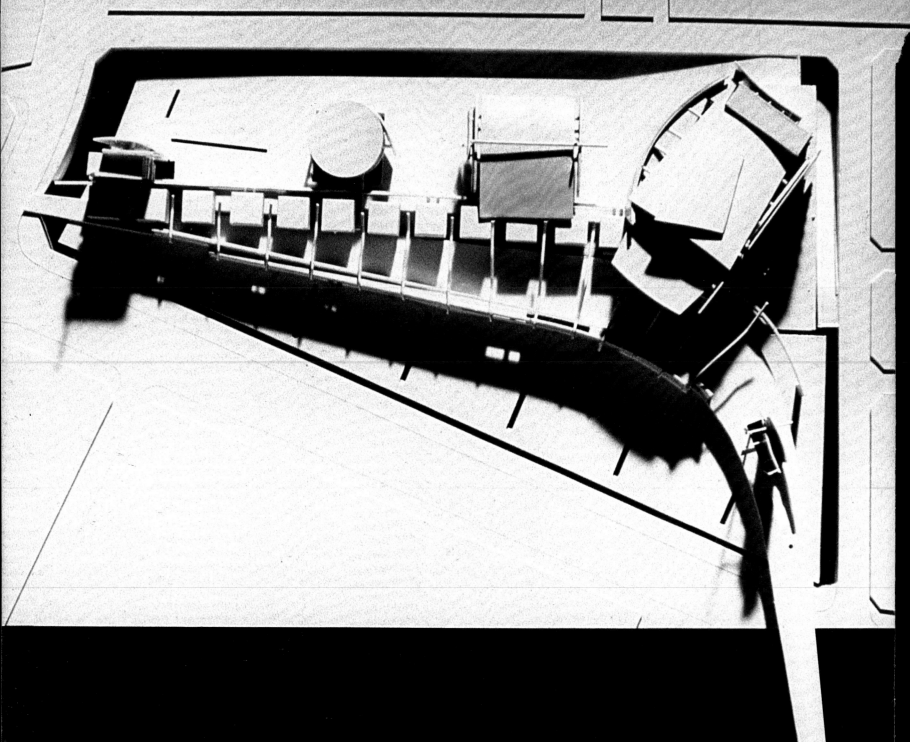

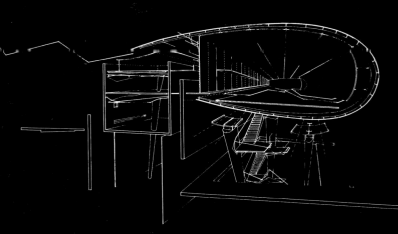

NARA CONVENTION CENTRE
Nara, Japan

The tradition of history, and the expectation of the future, is emphasised by the heritage of Nara as a place of culture and international commerce. The geography of the Silk Road and the nature of the city was analysed exposing traditional values, that are relevant to the contemporary issues of 'conference' and 'convention'.

The Japanese tradition of carrying food in a box, designed to house assorted dishes whilst maintaining a rigidity, was taken as a symbolic element of culture relevant to the 'symbiosis of history and the future'; it is a representation of the everyday life of a traveller. Taking the culture of the Silk Road, the nature of convention was explored as a place which harbours the private and public exchange. The proposal draws on these elements as devices in the city, which are developed both as ordering principles and objects.

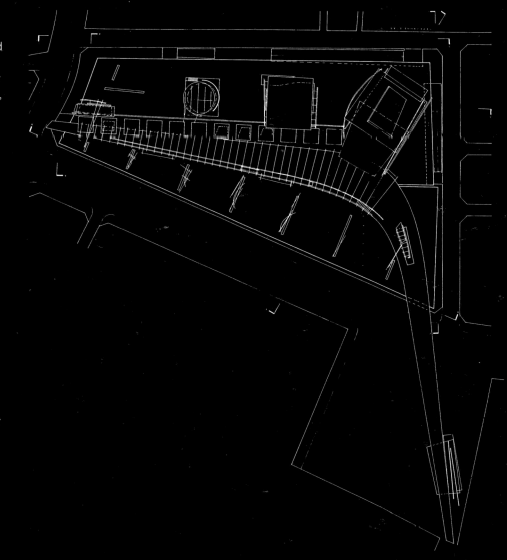

FROM ABOVE: Site plan; south elevation; east elevation; OPPOSITE: Internal perspective of intermediate hall

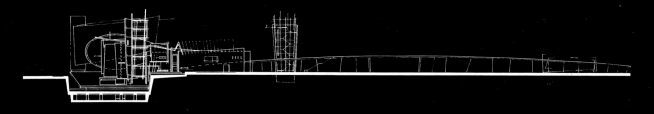

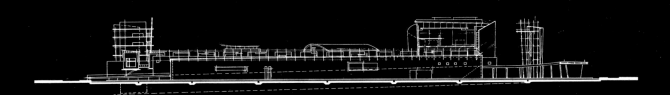

KLEIN DYTHAM
FASCINATING CULTURES

The term exile usually refers to a forced absence from one's country for political or monetary reasons. However, if the term can be used to describe an absence that was brought about by a fascination for a country – stimulated daily, for the past six years, by living and working there, regardless of whether economies were booming or receding – then we are exiles by choice. Voluntary exile allows visits home, and it is during these visits, and returns, that the true nature of a country and its culture become apparent.

Returning to London from Japan, makes one becomes aware of social mores that previously went unnoticed. One realizes that personal space in Tokyo during rush hour just does not exist, while in London it involves being able to read a broadsheet newspaper. The friendly London cabby now talks too much and drives an austere cab too aggressively. Yet, back in Japan the cab and driver seem terribly overdressed with cap, white gloves, coin-operated TV and even a mini 'genki' drink vending-machine on board. It is these contrasts that inform and flavour our work in Japan.

The Sanae Ozeki hair salon in Ginza, Tokyo, arranged around one central element, the mirror, was our first project in Japan. Conceived as a single sheet, the reflective sheet is acid-etched to create individual mirrors. In Japan mirrors appear everywhere, even in subway stations and telephone boxes, and people are constantly checking their image. The curved mirror playfully distorts this vanity.

Sanae Ozeki was our first glimpse at the construction process in Japan, and after only a few days the quality and precise nature of all construction work became evident, despite the high standards the design required. It was also interesting that the workers arrived in suits, changed on arrival and at the end

of everyday, meticulously tidied the site before changing back into their commuting clothes.

Throughout Japan, technology is embraced everywhere and by everyone; whether it is a domestic bath which can be filled remotely by phoning it on the way home, or office buildings with flavoured air-conditioning. This technological obsession inspires us to develop even wilder schemes, and our winning entry for the glass house of the future, the *Shinkenchiku* competition, followed in this spirit. Suspended in a bamboo grove, swaying gently in the breeze, the dynamism of the environment challenged the rigidity and tension of the glass. The house benefited from the shading and natural air-conditioning provided by the grove, but was also equipped with electrically heated glass and liquid crystal walls.

The Video-*Sento* is another project that illustrates this interest in technology whilst also maintaining a dialogue with Japanese culture. Awarded the *Kajima* Prize in 1993, this building is considered a single unit which has been sliced in two, revealing two large video screens. Images are projected from the opposite *sento*, or bathhouse, on to the frosted glass screens and can be viewed from both the building's interior and exterior. The old bathhouses are slowly becoming extinct, and the Video-*Sento* aims to make the younger generation discover this civilized culture. The videos represent a contemporary interpretation of the traditional panoramic landscapes that were displayed on the walls of original *sentos*.

Being 'exiled' in Japan is rather similar to being a child again, learning, discovering and experimenting in a new culture, but with the benefit of having an existing set of cultural notions with which to judge, compare and combine the new set.

Mark Dytham

OPPOSITE: Sanae Ozeki, Tokyo; ABOVE: Video-Sento, Space Design Review '93; OVERLEAF: Glass House 2001, Shinkenchiku/ JA competition

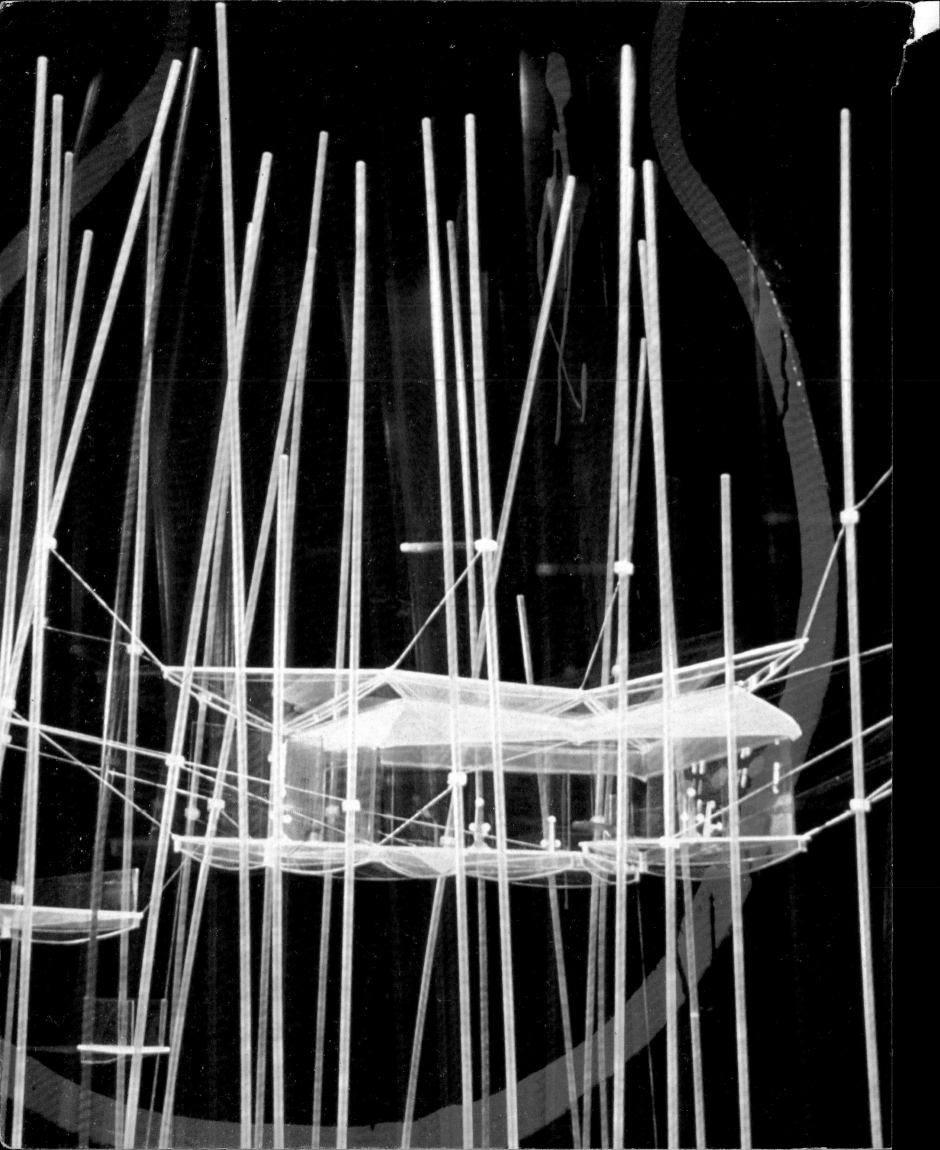